TEACHER'S MANUAL
Adventures in Phonics

Level B

A publication of
Christian Liberty Press
502 West Euclid Avenue
Arlington Heights, Illinois 60004
www.christianlibertypress.com

Written by Florence M. Lindstrom
Layout and editing by Edward J. Shewan
Copyediting by Belit M. Shewan
Cover design by Bob Fine

ISBN 978-1-930092-78-5
          1-930092-78-4

Printed in the United States of America

For the Teacher

The primary goal of phonics instruction is to help the student become a strong reader by teaching him the *sounds* made by individual letters and the combinations of letters. This will enable him to sound out an unlimited number of words. Emphasis should be placed upon teaching the *sound* of each letter and *not* its name. Only the *sounds* of the letters help us read words. Once your student understands the basic rules of phonics, the world of reading will open up to him. This will also enable him to be a good speller.

It is important for teachers to follow the instructions located in this **Teacher's Manual** as a preparation for the daily lessons in *Adventures in Phonics Level B*. Keep in mind that students learn at varying rates of speed depending on their previous schooling, their maturity, and the difficulty of the lesson. If your student has completed *Adventures in Phonics Level A*, then the first 129 pages will serve as a review and reinforcement of that workbook. If this, however, is the first exposure to learning the sounds of the letters and to reading, the student may need extra drill and review. In this case, the student should use the flashcards which can be removed from the back of this **Teacher's Manual.** Spend as much time as you feel necessary to help your student understand each lesson.

In the student's workbook, the pages have been perforated so that they can easily be removed to help the student in completing his work. All the student's work should be carefully saved for review purposes.

The two most important attributes of a phonics teacher are loving patience and caring perseverance. May the Lord grant you, the instructor, an abundant supply of both.

Florence Lindstrom

Christian Liberty Academy

Arlington Heights, IL

Page 1

Purpose

Teach the recognition, sound, and formation of the short vowel **a**.

Before class begins

1. Remove flashcard **A a** from the set at the back of this manual.

2. Open to the first page.

Lesson

Enthusiastically explain that the **A a** is one of the five vowels which are so important in reading. Vowels have several sounds, but the short sounds will be learned first. Ask the student to repeat the sound three times after you as you point at the three ways it is printed (A, a, and a). This sound is heard at the beginning of **a**-pple, **a**-nt, **a**-nswer. In the shaded box near the upper left-hand side of the page, the top letter shows how people print the capital or **upper-case** letter A—used at the beginning of a person's name such as Andrew or Anna. The bottom letter shows how people print the **lower-case** letter **a**.

Place the flashcard near the work area so it is seen as the page is being studied.

Follow directions and complete the lesson.

Page 2

Purpose

Teach the recognition, sound, and formation of the short vowel **e**.

Before class begins

1. Remove flashcard **E e** from the set at the back of this manual.

2. Open to the second page.

Lesson

Review the **A a** flashcard with your student saying it five times. Say the short sound of **E e** as you introduce that flashcard, having the student repeat it after you. Drill with both cards, listening to hear that the student can distinguish between the two sounds.

Have him repeat after you: **e**-gg, **e**-nd, **E**-mily, **e**-mpty, **e**-lephant, **e**-lbow, etc., taking additional examples from the worksheet if needed.

Follow the directions and complete the lesson.

Page 3

Purpose

Teach the recognition, sound, and formation of the short vowel **i**.

Before class begins

1. Remove flashcard **I i** from the set at the back of this manual.

2. Open to the new lesson.

Lesson

Review the **A a** and **E e** flashcards with your student, saying them five times. Say the short sound of **I i** as you introduce that flashcard, having the student repeat it after you. Drill with all three cards, listening to hear that the student can distinguish between the three sounds.

Have him repeat after you: **i**-nch, **i**-nvite, **i**-n, **i**-tch, **i**-nside, **i**-nner, etc., taking additional examples from the worksheet if needed.

Follow the directions as you have the student complete the lesson.

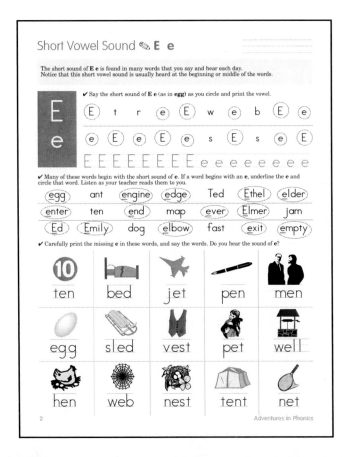

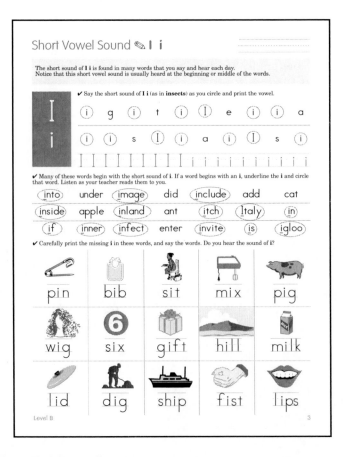

Page 4

Purpose

Teach the recognition, sound, and formation of the short vowel **o**.

Before class begins

1. Remove flashcard **O o** from the set at the back of this manual.

2. Open to the new lesson.

Lesson

Review the flashcards for **A a**, **E e**, and **I i**, listening closely to hear that the sounds are said correctly. Introduce the **O o** flashcard, saying the short sound of **O o**, which is heard at the beginning of O-ctober, o-n, o-bject, O-scar, and o-ctopus. Before the student begins to print the vowel **o**, explain that he should begin by thinking about the 2 on a clock and proceeding backward to the 2 again.

Follow the directions and complete the lesson.

Page 5

Purpose

Review the first four vowels and teach the recognition, sound, and formation of the short vowel **u**.

Before class begins

1. Remove flashcard **U u** from the set at the back of this manual.

2. Open to the new lesson.

Lesson

Review the **A a**, **E e**, **I i**, and **O o** flashcards. Introduce the **U u** shape and sound. You may want to test the student by having him point to the correct flashcard as you say words like the following: A-frica, **u**-s, **i**-nch, E-sther, A-dam, **o**-live, **e**-dge, **u**-nder, **a**-fter, **o**-nward, I-ndian, **u**-ncle, etc.

Follow the directions as you have the student complete the lesson.

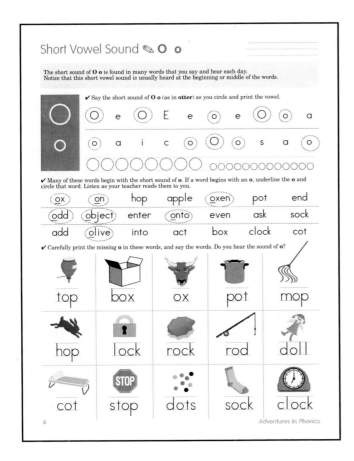

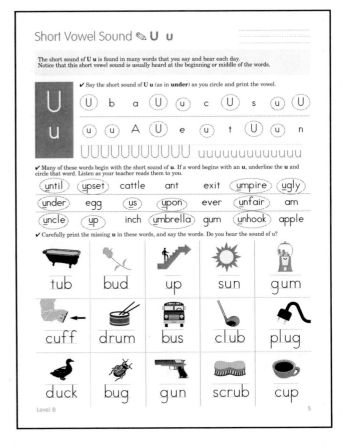

Page 6

Purpose

Teach the recognition, sound, and formation of the consonant **s**.

Before class begins

Open to the new lesson and have the flashcard **S s** ready to add to the short vowel flashcards.

Lesson

Briefly discuss that the letters belong in two different groups: **vowels** and **consonants**. The first consonant that will be learned is the **S s**. Some important words that begin with this consonant are: Saviour, Spirit, salvation, sin, scriptures, soul, and sermon.

Read the following sentences to your student:

Seven sandy sea gulls sat still on a silver sailboat.

See the six snails sleep silently on the soft sand at the sunny seaside.

Follow the directions and complete the top half of the page. Practice doing the bottom section orally so that the student will learn the beginning consonant/vowel sound before he tries to complete that section by himself.

After completing the lesson, spend additional drill time by "reading" **sa, se, si, so,** and **su.**

Page 7

Purpose

Teach the recognition, sound, and formation of the consonant **t**.

Before class begins

Open to the new lesson and have the flashcard **T t** ready.

Lesson

Begin the lesson by asking these questions: "How many toes do you have?" "What do we like to do on the telephone?" "What would be fun to sleep in out in the backyard?" "What needs to be on our suitcase to show that it belongs to us?" Show the **T t** flashcard and print it on the board, telling that letters are usually formed from the top.

Have the student repeat each of the following words and the sentence as you say them:

Testament, tower, tiger, tennis, Texas, teach, tabernacle, turkey, tooth, Tommy, Teresa, Tuesday

Ten timid turtles traveled toward a tall tunnel on Tuesday.

Follow the directions and complete the top half of the page. Practice doing the bottom section orally, so the student will learn the beginning consonant or vowel sound before he tries to complete that section by himself.

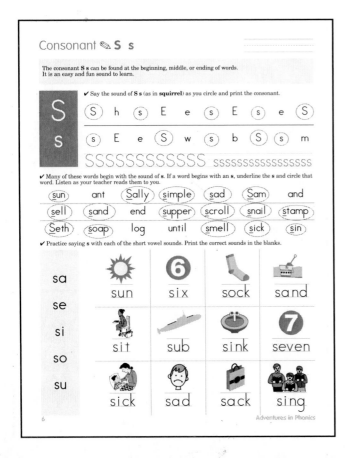

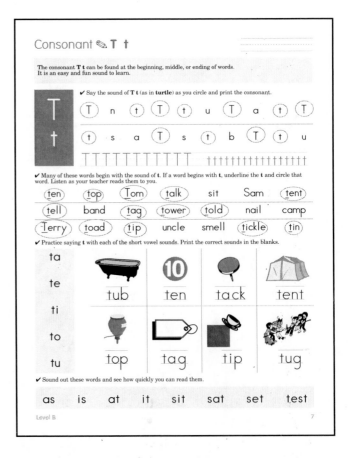

Page 8

Purpose

Teach the recognition, sound, and formation of the consonant **b**.

Before class begins

Open to the new lesson and have the flashcard **B b** ready to add to the short vowel flashcards.

Lesson

Ask the student, "What is the most important book that God wants us to read?" (Bible) "Yes, the **B**ible is the **b**est **b**ook." Show him the **B b** flashcard and tell him that this is the consonant that says that **b**eginning sound. Add this flashcard to the drill stack and have him practice saying them. Have your student repeat after you, as you say these wonderful things that God has given to us for a blessing: **b**anana, **b**erries, **b**utter, **b**eans, **b**ears, **b**eagle, and **b**est of all—**b**abies.

Help the student print these words:

b a t   b i t   b u t   s a t   s e t   s i t

Follow the directions and complete the top half of the page. Practice doing the bottom section orally, so the student will learn the beginning consonant/vowel sound before he tries to complete that section by himself.

Page 9

Purpose

Teach the recognition, sound, and formation of the consonant **h**.

Before class begins

Open to the new lesson and have the flashcard **H h** ready to add to the "known" flashcards.

Lesson

Ask the student, "Where will we live forever with Jesus if we love Him?" (Heaven). Tell him that each time we say this letter we let breath out of our mouth. Show him the **H h** flashcard and how to print the letter. Have him repeat after you as you say:

Happy **H**erman **h**as **h**undreds of **h**ealthy **h**ens in **h**is **h**en **h**ouse.

Herbert **h**elped **H**arvey **h**aul a **h**eavy **h**elicopter to the **h**angar.

Help your student to print these words on the board or paper.

h a t   h i t   h o t   h u t   h e n
h u b   t u b   b u s   s u b   s i t

Complete the page, working the bottom section orally before using a pencil.

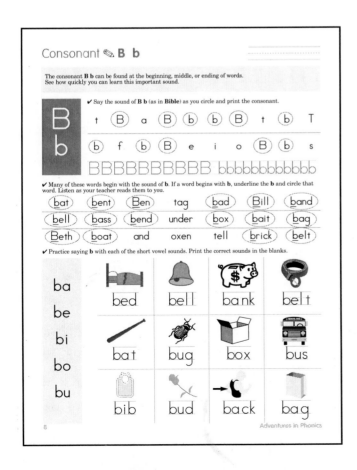

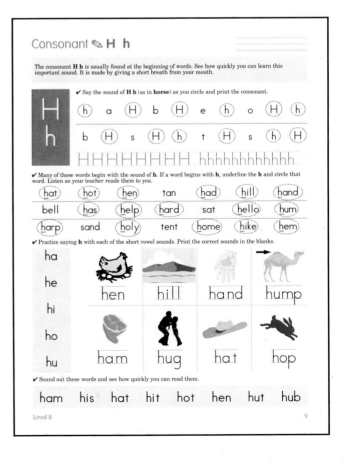

Page 10

Purpose

Teach the recognition, sound, and formation of the consonant **f**.

Before class begins

Open to the new lesson and have the flashcard **F f** ready to add to the "known" flashcards.

Lesson

Say: "Listen to the funny sound that comes out between our top teeth and bottom lip as this new sound is made. Fred and his father proudly flew their flag from the front porch for the Fourth of July. To have friends, one must be friendly."

Ask the student to listen for this sound at the end or in the middle of these words: leaf, calf, stuff, loaf, roof, coffee, muffin, puffing.

Teach the formation of this consonant, beginning from the top of the letter. Help the student to print the following words on a board or paper. If it is too difficult, print them slowly yourself to show how the words look. Be generous with encouragement and gentle with corrections.

> f a t   f i t   f a s t

Complete the page, working the bottom section orally before using a pencil.

Page 11

Purpose

Teach the recognition, sound, and formation of the consonant **m**.

Before class begins

Open to the new lesson and have the flashcard **M m** ready to add to the "known" flashcards.

Lesson

As you hold the **M m** flashcard, show with your lips how this consonant is formed by saying:

Mary's mother made meatballs on Monday.

Molly made a mess and must mop.

Many musicians played marvelous music at the

marriage of Michael and Martha.

Quickly drill all the flashcards. Help the student to print the following words as you slowly say them.

> m a t   a m   m o m   h a m   h e m
>
> m e t   h i m   h u m   m u s t   m u m

Complete the page, working the bottom section orally before using a pencil.

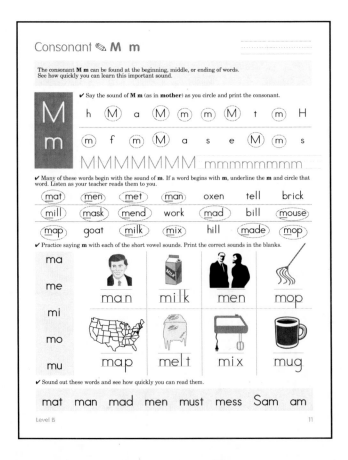

Page 12

Purpose

Teach the recognition, sound, and formation of the consonants **c** and **k**.

Before class begins

Open to the new lesson and have the flashcards **C c** and **K k** ready to learn.

Lesson

As you show these cards, say that both of these consonants can make the same sound. Read this sentence. Point at the words to show your student as you read this sentence.

God <u>c</u>reated all the <u>c</u>reatures such as the <u>c</u>ro<u>c</u>odile, <u>c</u>row, <u>k</u>iwi, <u>c</u>ougar, <u>c</u>ricket, <u>c</u>ondor, <u>c</u>o<u>c</u>katoo, <u>k</u>angaroo, <u>k</u>udu, <u>k</u>oala, <u>c</u>amel, <u>c</u>ow, <u>k</u>atydid, and <u>c</u>aterpillar.

The **k** usually makes the **k** sound if it is followed by **e** or **i** as in **key** and **king**.

The **c** usually makes the **k** sound if it is followed by **a**, **o**, or **u** as in **cat**, **cot**, and **cut**.

Complete the page, working the bottom section orally before using a pencil.

Page 13

Purpose

Teach the recognition, sound, and formation of the consonants **c** and **k**.

Before class begins

Open to the new lesson and have the flashcards **C c** and **K k** ready to learn.

Lesson

As you show these cards, say that both of these consonants can make the same sound. Read this sentence. Point at the words to show your student as you read this sentence.

God <u>c</u>reated all the <u>c</u>reatures such as the <u>c</u>ro<u>c</u>odile, <u>c</u>row, <u>k</u>iwi, <u>c</u>ougar, <u>c</u>ricket, <u>c</u>ondor, <u>c</u>o<u>c</u>katoo, <u>k</u>angaroo, <u>k</u>udu, <u>k</u>oala, <u>c</u>amel, <u>c</u>ow, <u>k</u>atydid, and <u>c</u>aterpillar.

The **k** usually makes the **k** sound if it is followed by **e** or **i** as in **key** and **king**.

The **c** usually makes the **k** sound if it is followed by **a**, **o**, or **u** as in **cat**, **cot**, and **cut**.

Complete the page, working the bottom section orally before using a pencil.

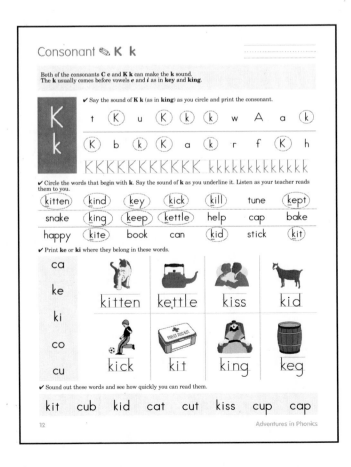

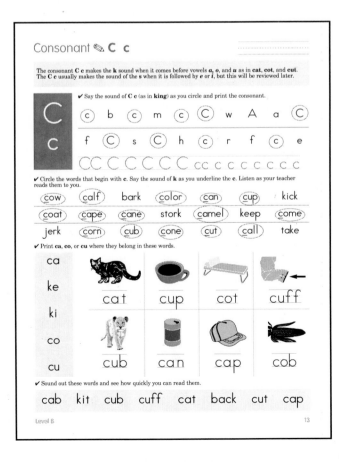

Page 14

Purpose

Teach the recognition, sound, and formation of the consonant **d**.

Before class begins

Have the new lesson and flashcard **D d** ready.

Lesson

Quickly drill all the consonant flashcards, especially noting the **b** flashcard. Show the **d** flashcard as you read these sentences:

Daniel **did** not **d**isobey and was **d**elivered by Go**d** from being **d**estroyed by lions in the **d**en.

Davi**d**'s **d**og **d**igs **d**eep holes in the **d**irt.

Spend time helping the student to learn the difference between **d** and **b**.

Slowly dictate these words or print them yourself for the student to read.

dot   dim   did   sad   bad

mad   dad   had   dab   sob

Complete the page, working the bottom section orally before using a pencil.

Page 15

Purpose

Teach the recognition, sound, and formation of the consonant **j**.

Before class begins

Have the new lesson and flashcard **J j** ready.

Lesson

As you show the **J j** flashcard say: "Our new sound is heard at the beginning of Jesus." Ask the student to repeat after you some of the other names that come from the Bible:

Jehovah, Joseph, Joshua, Jonah, James, Jacob, Jesse, John, Jeremiah, Judah, Joel, Jedediah, Jael, Jezebel, Jehoshaphat, and Job.

Also read:

January, June, and July are months.

Jeremiah likes to eat Jell-o, jam, and jelly.

Julie joyfully joined Janet to jump rope.

Slowly dictate these words or print them yourself for the student to read.

jet   jam   job   just   jab   jell

Complete the page, working the bottom section orally before using a pencil.

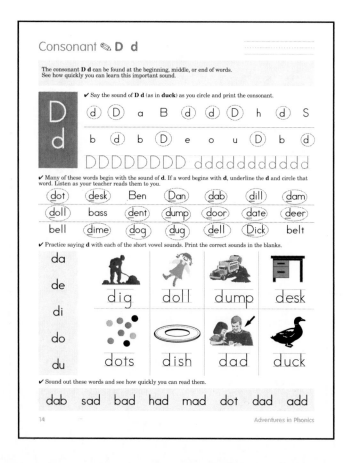

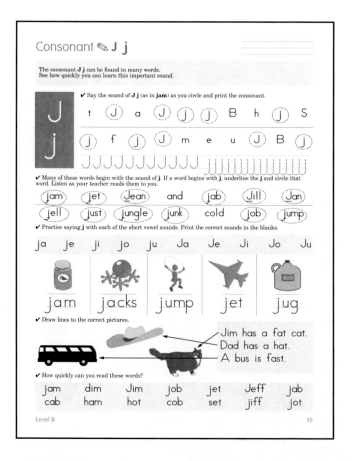

Page 16

Purpose

Teach the recognition, sound, and formation of the consonant **r**.

Before class begins

Have the new lesson and flashcard **R r** ready.

Lesson

As you show the **R r** flashcard, have the student repeat after you:

Ruth was a reaper.

Ralph's red roses are rare.

Robert's rubber raft rocked and made a ripple on the river.

Richard saw a rainbow above his roof.

Rosa's ruby ring rolled right under a round rock.

Teach how the letters **R r** should be printed.

Can your student print these words?

ran red rug rock rat rim

Complete the page, working the bottom section orally before using a pencil.

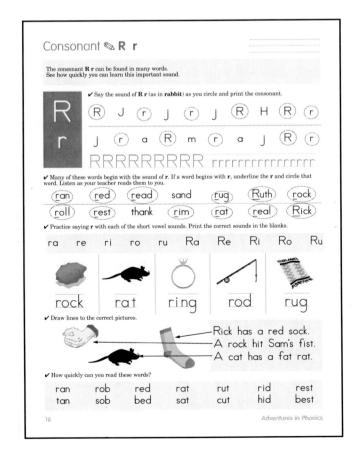

Page 17

Purpose

Teach the recognition, sound, and formation of the consonant **g**.

Before class begins

Have the new lesson and flashcard **G g** ready.

Lesson

As you show the **G g** flashcard, say: "Our great and gracious God made every good thing."

Ask the students to repeat after you:

Grace gave gold gifts to the good girls.

Gray geese got goodies from the garden.

Grant's goat gobbled green grapes and grass.

After you teach how to print **G g**, help the student to print these words:

God gift get gas got
hug tag big beg tug

Complete the page, working the bottom section orally before using a pencil.

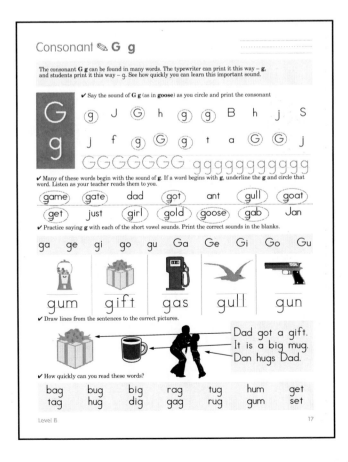

Page 18

Purpose

Teach the recognition, sound, and formation of the consonant l.

Before class begins

Have the new lesson and flashcard L l ready.

Lesson

As you introduce this sound, ask the student to repeat these sentences after you:

The Lord is my light.
I love the law of my Lord.
The Bible is a lamp and a light for my life.

Also say:

Lois likes licorice and lemon lollipops.
Larry laughed loudly as his lambs leaped lightly over leaves on the lawn.

An important lesson to teach is that the letter l is *doubled* when it is at the end of short vowel words. Write these words for reading:

hill   mill   fill   doll   dull

sell   tell   fell   bell   gull

Complete the page, working the bottom section orally before using a pencil.

Page 19

Purpose

Teach the recognition, sound, and formation of the consonant n.

Before class begins

Have the new lesson and flashcard N n ready.

Lesson

Say this sound several times as you teach how to print it.

Ask your student, "What rhyming words beginning with the letter n answer the following sentences?"

A cat on my lap   Ned bought a pickle
Took a long (nap).   For just one (nickel).

The white purse   Nancy smelled a rose
Belongs to a (nurse).   With her (nose).

Help the student spell these words on a paper or board:

nut   net   not   nap   ten   tan

Complete the page, working the bottom section orally before using a pencil.

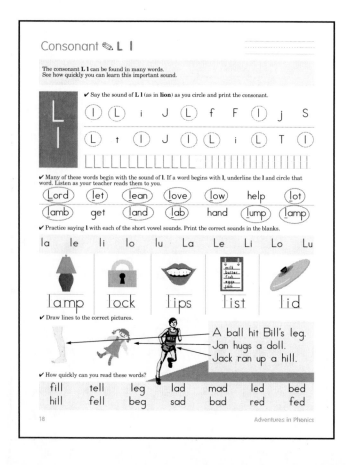

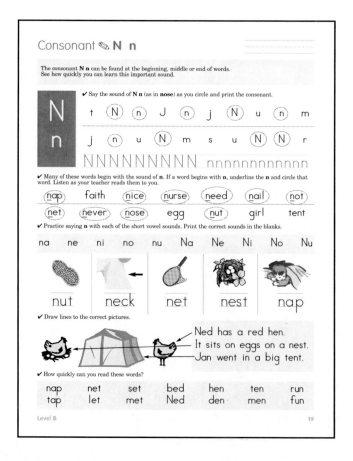

Page 20

Purpose

Teach the recognition, sound, and formation of the consonant **w**.

Before class begins

Have the new lesson and flashcard **W w** ready.

Lesson

Show the **W w** flashcard and say that this letter is fun to draw—going down, up, down, up. Have your student repeat the following sentences after you:

God made our **w**onderful **w**orld.

Wendy and **W**illiam **w**atched a **w**oman **w**ash **w**ide **w**indows **w**ith **w**ater from the **w**ell on **W**ednesday in **W**est **W**ellington.

Ask him to listen and say after you these places that begin with the consonant **w**: **W**yoming, **W**innipeg, **W**illiamsburg, **W**ittenberg, **W**ales, and **W**inston.

After the student practices printing **W w**, help him to print these words:

wet well will wag went
web wed wig win west

Complete the page, working the bottom section orally before using a pencil.

Note that *win* or *won* may be used under the runner in the middle of page 20, even though this sound of **o** has not been taught yet.

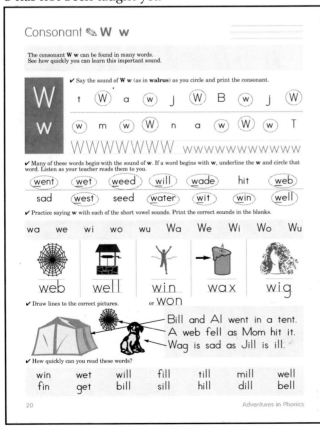

Page 21

Purpose

Teach the recognition, sound, and formation of the consonant **p**.

Before class begins

Have the new lesson and flashcard **P p** ready.

Lesson

As you show this flashcard say, "Our lips come together as we begin to make this sound. We **p**raise God in our **p**rayers for His **p**erfect **p**lans."

Have the student listen closely as you say:

Peter and **P**aul **p**acked **p**lenty of food for a **p**icnic in the **p**ark in **P**ennsylvania. They brought **p**op, **p**ickles, **p**otato chips, **p**eanuts, **P**opsicles, **p**ears, **p**izza, **p**retzels, **p**eaches, **p**umpkin **p**ie, and **p**opcorn.

Teach the student how to print **P p** and help him to print these words on a paper or board.

pan pet pig pad pill
map mop cup top dip

Complete the page, working the bottom section orally before using a pencil.

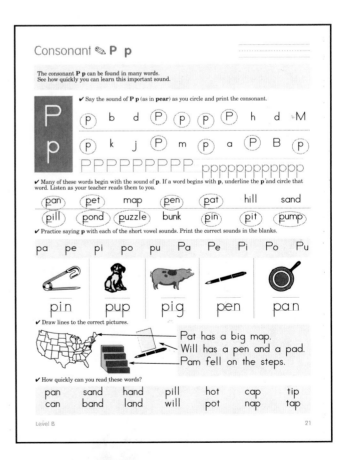

Page 22

Purpose

Teach the recognition, sound, and formation of the consonant **v**.

Before class begins

Have the new lesson and flashcard **V v** ready.

Lesson

As you show the **V v** flashcard and say its sound, have the student listen and slowly repeat:

Victoria and Virginia visited Valerie's vineyard and vegetable garden in a vacant lot in the village down in a valley.

Verna put violets and vines in a very nice vase and vacuumed the veranda.

Victor put his violin into his van.

Help the student to print these words:

van   vest   vet   vast   vent

Complete the page, working the bottom section orally before using a pencil.

Page 23

Purpose

Teach the recognition, sound, and formation of the consonant **q**.

Before class begins

Have the new lesson and flashcard **Qu qu** ready.

Lesson

As you show this flashcard, teach that in English the consonant **q** is always followed by the vowel **u**. Have the student repeat after you as you say these words:

quest   quart   quail
quick   quill   quit

Complete the page, working the bottom section orally before using a pencil.

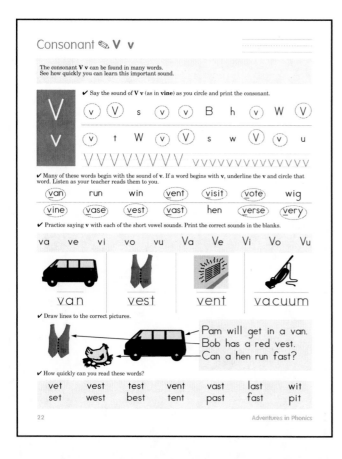

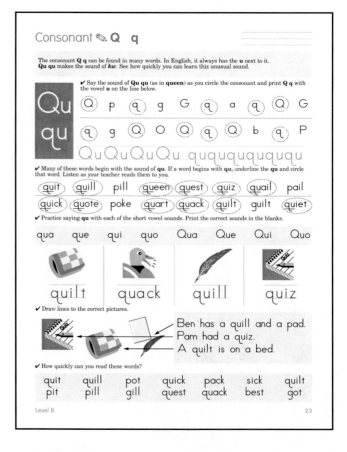

Page 24

Purpose

Teach the recognition, sound, and formation of the consonant **y**.

Before class begins

Have the new lesson and flashcard **Y y** ready.

Lesson

Show the **Y y** flashcard and say its sound. You may want to explain in this lesson that **y** is a consonant at the beginning of words, but it is a vowel when it is at the end of words. This will be taught in a later lesson. Have your student repeat these sentences after you:

You should remember **your** Creator in the days of **your youth**.

The **young** girl made a scarf with **yellow yarn**.

The **yolk** of an egg is **yellow**.

Yes, you may play in the **yard** with **your yo-yo**.

Yesterday we ate **yogurt** on a **yacht**.

Help the student to print these words:

yes   yak   yet   yum   yam

Complete the page, working the bottom section orally before using a pencil.

Page 25

Purpose

Teach the recognition, sound, and formation of the consonant **x**.

Before class begins

Have the new lesson and flashcard **X x** ready.

Lesson

Show the **X x** flashcard and explain that it usually is at the end of words. It has the sound made by saying the sounds of **k** and **s** together as in: bo**x** and mi**x**. Print these words on the board or a paper as you ask the student to read them:

ax   tax   fix   six   fox
ox   mix   box   wax   fax

Complete the page, working the bottom section orally before using a pencil.

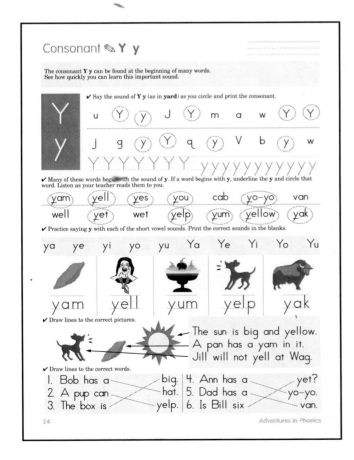

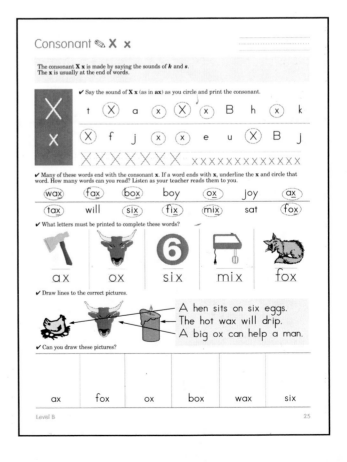

Page 26

Purpose

Teach the recognition, sound, and formation of the consonant z.

Before class begins

Have the new lesson and flashcard Z z ready.

Lesson

Show the Z z flashcard and say that it is the sound that a bee makes. We can hear it at the beginning of zag, zig, zigzag, zoom, and zip code.

Ask these questions:

1. Where can we see many wild animals? (zoo)

2. What animal looks like a horse wearing striped pajamas? (zebra)

3. What helps to close up your jacket? (zipper)

4. What short man was a tax collector who became a Christian? (Zacchaeus)

5. What number is like the shape of a circle? (zero)

Help the student print these words:

zap   zip   zest   zag

Have the student complete the page.

Page 27

Purpose

To give practice in reading short vowel words.

Lesson

Help the student to print these words:

at   pen   tip   pop   rub

sat   hen   rip   hop   tub

Discuss the directions and have the student complete the lesson.

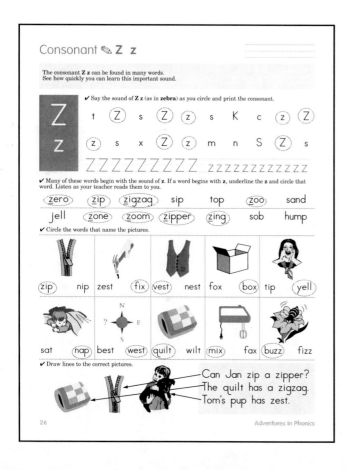

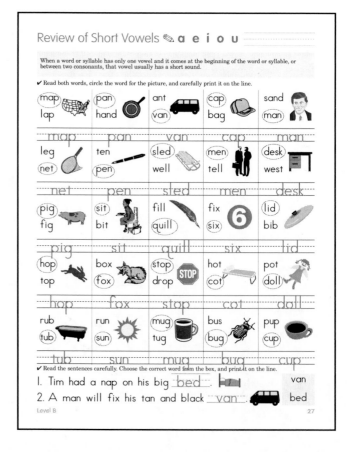

Page 28

Purpose
To give practice in reading and printing short vowel **a** words.

Lesson
Have the student practice reading the list of short vowel **a** words on Charts 1 and 2 (page 215 in the workbook). The student should be able to clearly read Chart 1 before starting on Chart 2. (Chart 2 may be covered at a later time.) It may go slowly at first, but give encouragement and compliments whenever possible.

It would give your student a good introduction and extra practice if you heard him read the lists in the lesson and orally answer the sentences before he does the work independently.

Page 29

Purpose
To give practice in reading and printing short vowel **e** words.

Lesson
Have the student practice reading the list of short vowel **e** words on Chart 3 (page 215 in the workbook). Do not be impatient if it goes slowly at first. Try to give encouragement and compliments whenever possible.

Listen to the student read the lists in the lesson and orally answer the sentences before he does the work independently.

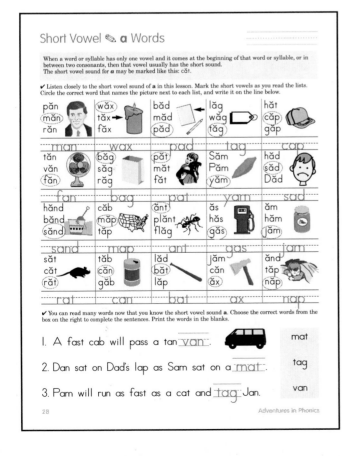

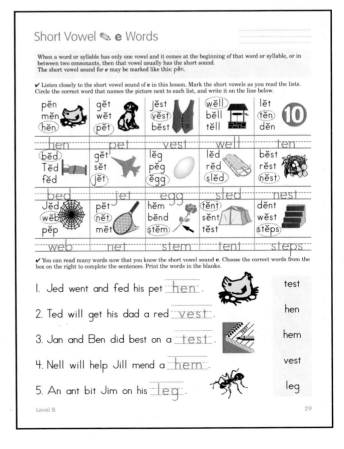

Page 30

Purpose

To give practice in reading and printing short vowel **i** words.

Lesson

Have the student practice reading the list of short vowel **i** words on Chart 4 (page 216 in the workbook). Be patient as you listen. Give encouragement and compliments.

To give your student extra practice, listen to him read the lists in the lesson and orally answer the sentences before he does the work independently.

Page 31

Purpose

To give practice in reading and printing short vowel **o** words.

Lesson

Have the student practice reading the list of short vowel **o** words on Chart 5 (page 216 in the workbook). Patiently listen as you encourage and commend.

To give your student extra practice, listen to him read the lists in the lesson and orally answer the sentences before he does the work independently.

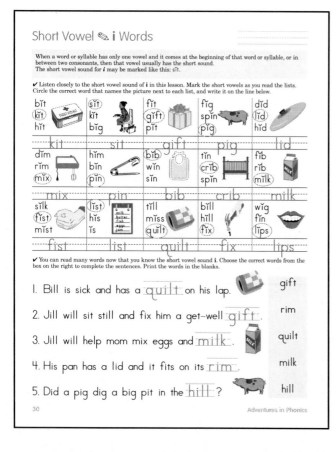

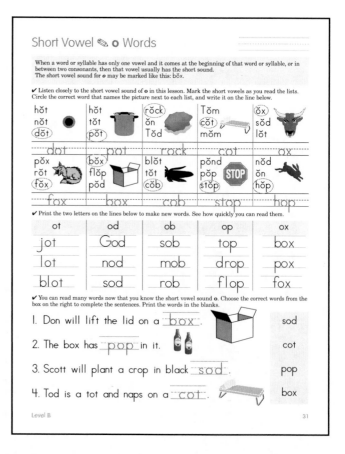

Page 32

Purpose

To give practice in reading and printing short vowel **u** words. To learn about the vowel **o** sometimes having the short vowel **u** sound.

Lesson

Have the student practice reading the list of short vowel **u** words on Chart 6 (page 216 in the workbook). Patiently listen as you encourage and commend.

Introduce the short sound of **u** that is made by the vowel **o**, as in mother, son, brother, etc. Listen and help as your student reads the words on Chart 18 (page 220 in the workbook).

Listen as your student reads the lists in the lesson and orally answers the sentences before he does the work independently.

Page 33

Purpose

To teach words beginning and ending with consonant blends. To cause the student to notice two or three consonants sounding or blending together.

Lesson

Print the following blends and words on the board or paper and listen to your student say them. You may choose to have them read from this key. These are just some of the blends.

bl nd	fl	gl	pl nt
blend	flag	glass	plant
sl pt	ft	cr st	gr sp
slept	gift	crust	grasp
scr	sq (u)	str	lk
scrub	squid	strap	milk

Discuss the lesson orally before it is completed independently.

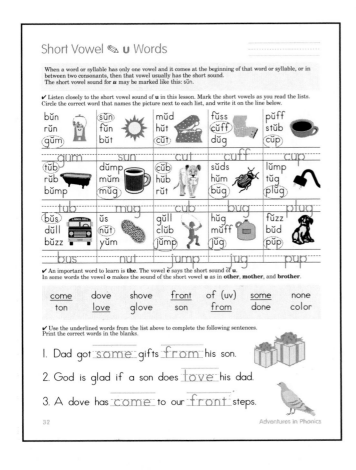

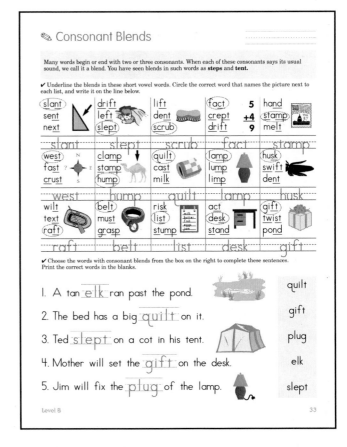

Page 34

Purpose
To teach that in short vowel words, usually the ending consonants **s**, **l**, **f**, and **z** will be *doubled*.

Lesson
Print the following words on the board or paper and listen to your student say them. You may choose to have them read from this key.

grass   bell   fizz   buzz

glass   mess   doll   cuff

Listen as your student gives the answers to the lesson orally before he completes it independently.

Page 35

Purpose
To teach that short vowel words ending with the **k** sound is made with **ck**.

Lesson
Print the following words on the board or paper and listen to your student say them. You may choose to have them read from this key.

sack   neck   sock   cluck

crack   pick   flock   back

peck   stick   duck   kick

Have your student read the **ck** words on Chart 7 (page 217 in the workbook).

Listen as he gives the answers to the lesson orally before completing it independently.

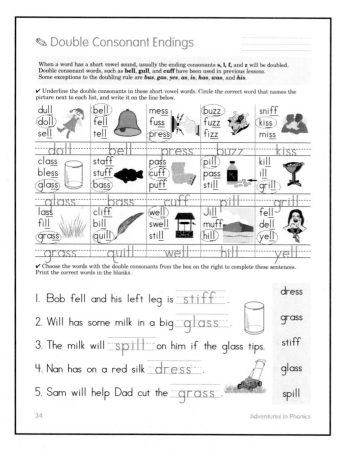

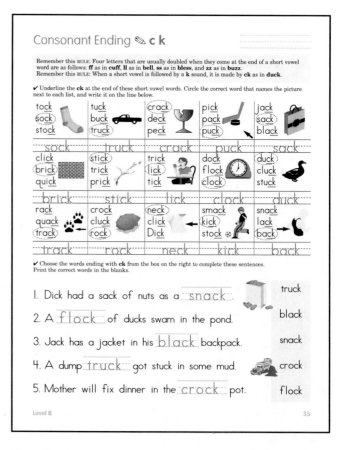

Page 36

Purpose
To teach the sounds made by the letters **ng** and **nk** at the end of short vowel words.

Lesson
Print the following words on the board or paper and listen closely to hear if your student says them correctly. You may choose to have them read from this key.

bang   sing   trunk   blank

sang   sung   dunk   sank

Listen as your student reads all the words on the lists and gives the answers to the lesson orally before he completes it independently.

Page 37

Purpose
To review short vowel words which end with **ss**, **ll**, **ff**, **zz** and **ck**.

Lesson
Have your student read Chart 7 (page 217 in the workbook) with short vowel words ending with **ck** and review the rule regarding the ending consonants **ss**, **ll**, **ff**, and **zz**. These words can be found on the short vowel Charts 2, 3, 4, and 6 (pages 215 and 216 in the workbook). Is he able to read the words quickly? Maybe he needs to try again at a later time.

Listen as your student reads the sentences and words on the lists and gives the answers to the lesson orally before he completes it independently.

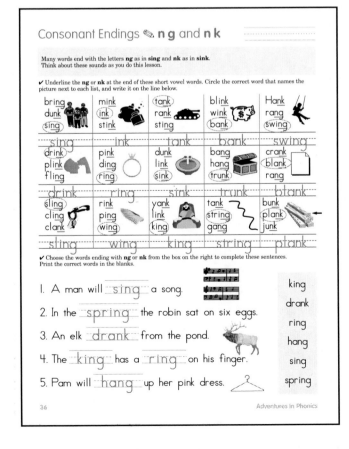

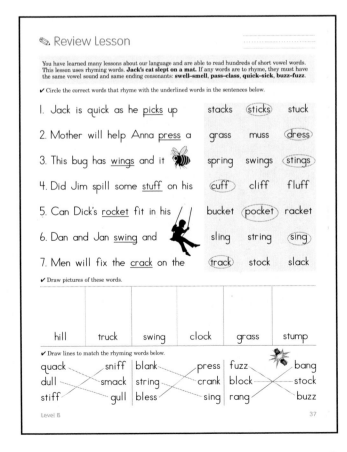

Page 38

Purpose
To teach words with sounds made by the digraphs **sh** and **ch**.

Lesson
Print the following words on the board or paper and listen closely to hear if your student says them correctly. You may choose to have them read from this key.

sh

ship shell shed rash fish

ch

chip chap chin lunch such

Practice reading the words with the digraphs **sh** and **ch** on Chart 8 (page 217 in the workbook). Also, you may want to use the flashcards for these digraphs.

Listen as your student reads all of the words on the lists and gives the answers to the lesson orally before he completes it independently.

Page 39

Purpose
To teach words with the digraphs **th** and **wh**.

Lesson
Print the following words on the board or paper and listen closely to hear if your student says them correctly. You may choose to have them read from this key.

The digraph **th** has two sounds:

th   as in   this
then   that   than   them   the

th   as in   thin
think thick Beth math bath

wh   as in   whip
when whip what whim why

Practice reading the **th** and **wh** words on Chart 9 (page 217 in the workbook). Also, you may want to use the flashcards for these digraphs.

Listen as your student reads all of the words on the lists and gives the answers to the lesson orally before he completes it independently.

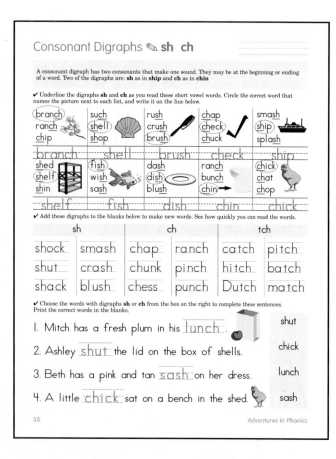

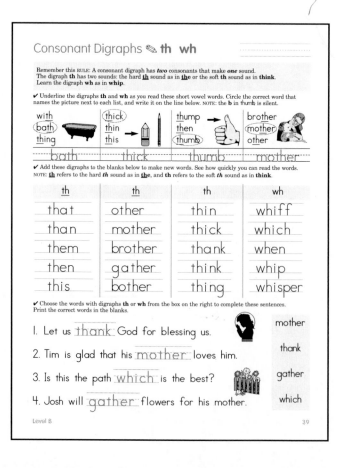

Page 40

Purpose
To teach the long vowel sound of **a**.

Lesson
Be familiar with the directions on the workbook page as you explain the difference between a short vowel sound and a long vowel sound. By now the student should know the main five vowels—**a**, **e**, **i**, **o**, and **u**. Say the long vowel rule several times, having it repeated after you say it.

Study the long vowel **a** words on Charts 10 and 11 (page 218 in the workbook), perhaps reading Chart 10 with this lesson and the Chart 11 with the next lesson. Also use the long vowel **a** flashcard.

Give special attention to the first exercise which compares the short and long vowel words.

Listen as your student reads all of the words on the lists and gives the answers to the lesson orally before he completes it independently.

Some lessons may take a longer time than others, but it is important that the student understands what is being taught. It is better that a second day be spent on a lesson, if there is uncertainty, than to go on and become more confused.

Page 41

Purpose
To teach the long vowel sound of **a**.

Lesson
Review the directions on the workbook page as you discuss the difference between a short vowel sound and a long vowel sound. Does the student remember the long vowel rule? Say it several times, having it repeated after you say it.

Study the rest of the long vowel **a** words on Chart 11 (page 218 in the workbook) or review both Charts 10 and 11 if the student knows them from the previous lesson. Also use the long vowel **a** flashcard.

Listen as your student reads all of the words on the lists and gives the answers to the lesson orally before he completes it independently.

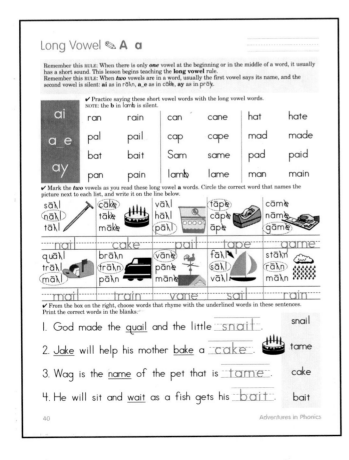

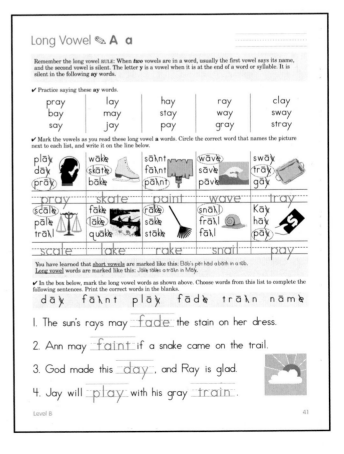

Page 42

Purpose
To teach the long vowel sound of **e**.

Lesson
Be familiar with the directions on the workbook page as you explain the difference between a short vowel sound and a long vowel sound. Say the long vowel rule several times, having it repeated after you say it.

Study the long vowel **e** words on Charts 12 and 13 (pages 218 and 219 in the workbook), perhaps reading Chart 12 with this lesson and Chart 13 with the next lesson. Also use the long vowel **e** flashcard.

Give special attention to the first exercise which compares the short and long vowel words.

Listen as your student reads all of the words on the lists and gives the answers to the lesson orally before he completes it independently.

Page 43

Purpose
To teach the long vowel sound of **e**.

Lesson
Review the directions on the workbook page as you explain the difference between a short vowel sound and a long vowel sound. Discuss the long vowel rule, asking the student to tell it to you.

Study the rest of the long vowel **e** words on Chart 13 or review both Charts 12 and 13 (pages 218 and 219 in the workbook) if the student knows them from the previous lesson. Also use the long vowel **e** flashcard.

Listen as your student reads all of the words on the lists and gives the answers to the lesson orally before he completes it independently.

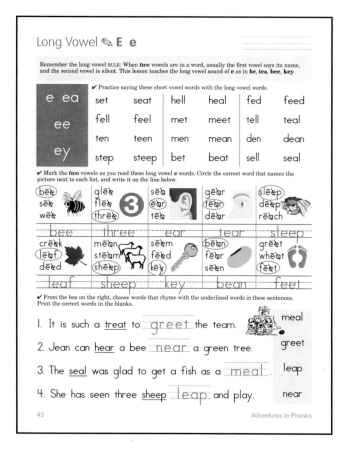

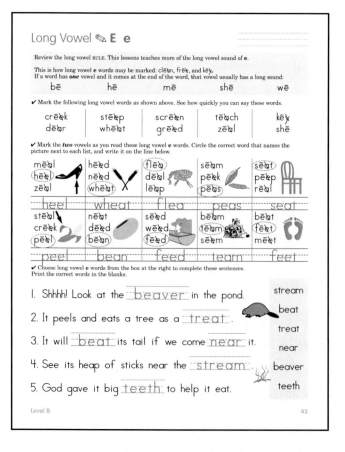

Page 44

Purpose
To teach the long vowel sound of **i**.

Lesson
Be familiar with the directions on the workbook page as you explain the difference between a short vowel sound and a long vowel sound. Say the long vowel rule several times, having it repeated after you say it.

Study the long vowel **i** words on Charts 14 and 15 (page 219 in the workbook), perhaps reading Chart 14 with this lesson and Chart 15 with the next lesson. Also use the long vowel **i** flashcard.

Give special attention to the first exercise that compares the short and long vowel words.

Listen as your student reads all of the words on the lists and gives the answers to the lesson orally before he completes it independently.

Page 45

Purpose
To teach the long vowel sound of **i**.

Lesson
Review the directions on the workbook page as you explain the difference between a short vowel sound and a long vowel sound. Discuss the long vowel rule, asking the student to say it to you.

Study the rest of the long vowel **i** words on Chart 15 (page 219 in the workbook) or review both Charts 14 and 15 if the student knows them from the previous lesson. Also use the long vowel **i** flashcard.

Listen as your student reads all of the words on the lists and gives the answers to the lesson orally before he completes it independently.

Note that the **s** can make the **z** sound in some words. Explain to your student that the **s** in *rise* and *wise* makes the sound of **z**.

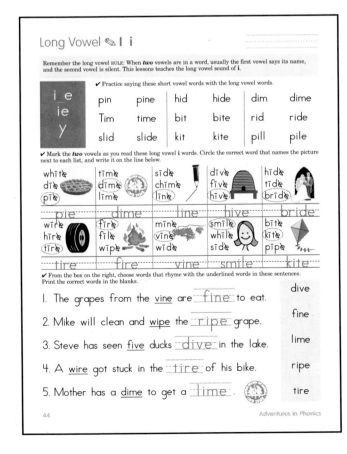

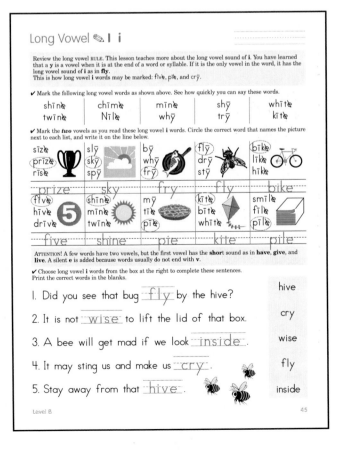

Page 46

Purpose

To teach the long vowel sound of **o**.

Lesson

Be familiar with the directions on the workbook page as you explain the difference between a short vowel sound and a long vowel sound. Say the long vowel rule several times, having it repeated after you say it.

Study the long vowel **o** words on Charts 16 and 17 (page 220 in the workbook), perhaps reading Chart 16 with this lesson and Chart 17 with the next lesson. Also use the long vowel **o** flashcard.

Give special attention to the first exercise which compares the short and long vowel words.

Listen as your student reads all of the words on the lists and gives the answers to the lesson orally before he completes it independently.

Note that the **s** can make the **z** sound in some words. Explain to your student that the **s** in *pose, rose, chose,* and *nose* makes the sound of **z**.

Page 47

Purpose

To teach the long vowel sound of **o**.

Lesson

Review the directions on the workbook page as you explain the difference between a short vowel sound and a long vowel sound. Discuss the long vowel rule, asking the student to say it to you.

Study the rest of the long vowel **o** words on Chart 17 (page 220 in the workbook) or review both Charts 16 and 17 if the student knows them from the previous lesson. Also use the long vowel **o** flashcard.

Listen as your student reads all of the words on the lists and gives the answers to the lesson orally before he completes it independently.

Note that the **s** can make the **z** sound in some words. Explain to your student that the **s** in *nose, rose,* and *hose* makes the sound of **z**.

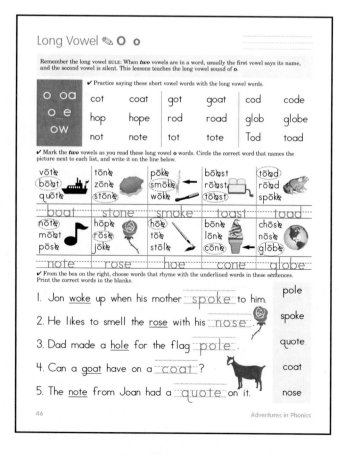

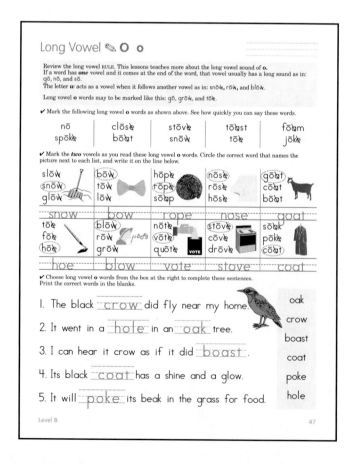

Page 48

Purpose
To teach the long vowel sound of **u**.

Lesson
Be familiar with the directions on the workbook page as you explain the difference between a short vowel sound and a long vowel sound. Say the long vowel rule several times, having it repeated after you say it.

Study the long vowel **u** words on Chart 19 (page 221 in the workbook), perhaps reading half of them with this lesson and the other half with the next lesson. Also use the long vowel **u** flashcard.

Give special attention to the first exercise which compares the short and long vowel words.

Listen as your student reads all of the words on the lists and gives the answers to the lesson orally before he completes it independently.

Note that the **s** can make the **z** sound in some words. Explain to your student that the **s** in *use* and *fuse* makes the sound of **z**.

Also note that sentence #5 at the bottom of page 48 may also read: "The doll has on a **cute** hat...."

Page 49

Purpose
To teach the long vowel sound of **u**.

Lesson
Review the directions on the workbook page as you explain the difference between a short vowel sound and a long vowel sound. Discuss the long vowel rule, asking the student to say it to you.

Study the rest of the long vowel **u** words on Chart 19 (page 221 in the workbook). Also use the long vowel **u** flashcard.

Listen as your student reads all of the words on the lists and gives the answers to the lesson orally before he completes it independently.

Note that the **s** can make the **z** sound in some words. Explain to your student that the **s** in *use* makes the sound of **z**.

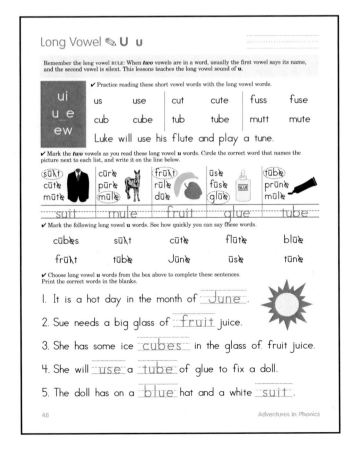

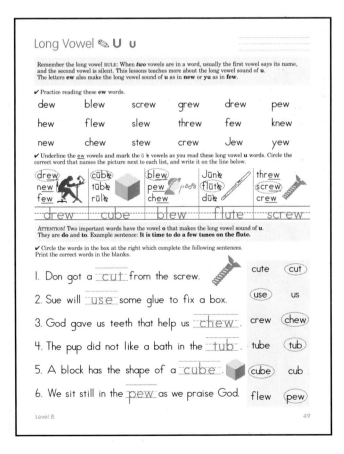

Page 50

Purpose
To review words that have long or short vowels.

Lesson
Say the long vowel rule, having it repeated after you say it.

Read all of the long vowel **a** words on Charts 10 and 11 (page 218 in the workbook).

Review the short vowel sounds **a e i o u**, with special attention to the short vowel **a**. Do you remember the rule that says there is only *one* vowel in short vowel words?

Listen as your student reads the words on the list and gives the answers to the lesson orally before he completes it independently.

Page 51

Purpose
To review words that have long or short vowels.

Lesson
Say the long vowel rule, having it repeated after you say it.

Read all of the long vowel **e** words on Charts 12 and 13 (pages 218 and 219 in the workbook).

Review the short vowel sounds **a e i o u**, especially the short vowel **e**. Review the rule that says there is only *one* vowel in short vowel words.

Listen as your student reads the words on the list and gives the answers to the lesson orally before he completes it independently.

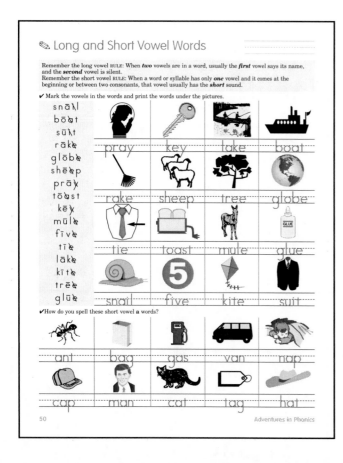

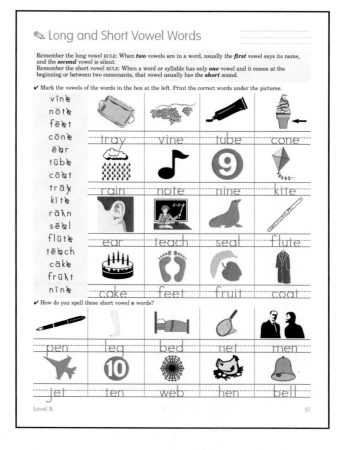

Page 52

Purpose
To review words that have long or short vowels.

Lesson
Say the long vowel rule, having it repeated after you say it. Read all of the long vowel **i** and **u** words on Charts 14 and 15 (page 219 in the workbook), and Chart 19 (page 221).

To give practice on what the lesson includes, print the following boxes on the board or paper and ask your student to use them as guides and print the words under the correct column as you pronounce them one at a time.

a_e	ee	i_e	o_e	u_e	ay

free   cone   way   cake   tube

cute   mine   tape   pray   rose

take   feet   tune   kite   tree

For more words, refer to the long vowel charts.

Review the short vowel rule and short vowel **i** sound before doing the bottom exercise.

Check the words and have the student correct any errors as soon as he completes the lesson.

Page 53

Purpose
To review words that have long or short vowels.

Lesson
Say the long vowel rule, having it repeated after you say it. Read the long vowel **o** words on Charts 16 and 17 (page 220 in the workbook).

To help introduce the lesson, put the following boxes on the board or paper and have your student say them until you feel that he knows them. Print the words and have him circle the vowel sounds he sees in each word before he reads the word.

ui	ai	oa	ea	ew	ow

heat   coat   few   soap   pail

slow   suit   meal   flow   seal

new   fail   main   chew   toad

If you want to add more words, refer to the long vowel charts.

Review the short vowel rule and short vowel **o** sound before doing the bottom exercise.

Check the work and have the student correct any errors as soon as he completes the lesson.

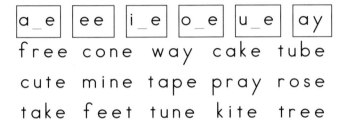

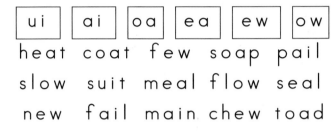

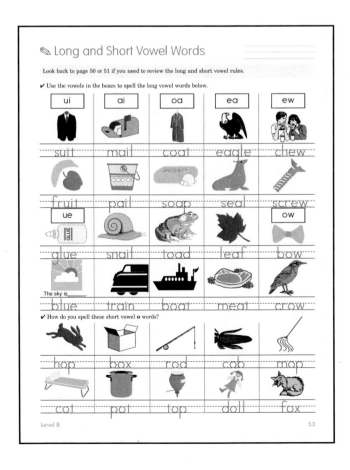

Page 54

Purpose

To teach the rule that a single **i** usually is short, except when followed by **ld**, **nd**, and **gh**. The **gh** is silent. To review short vowel words ending with **ck**.

Lesson

Ask the student to read the words on Chart 21 (page 221 in the workbook). Review the rule on Chart 7 (page 217 in the workbook) about short vowel words ending with the **ck**.

Listen as the student reads all of the words on the lists in the lesson and gives the answers to the lesson orally before he completes it independently.

Page 55

Purpose

To teach the rule that a single **o** may have the long vowel sound when followed by two consonants such as **ld**, **st**, **th**, **ll**, and **lt**. To review short vowel words ending with double consonants **ff**, **ll**, **ss**, and **zz**.

Lesson

Ask the student to read the words on Chart 22 (page 222 in the workbook). Review the rule about doubling the consonants **ff**, **ll**, **ss**, and **zz** at the end of short vowel words.

Listen as the student reads all of the words on the lists and gives the answers to the lesson orally before he completes it independently.

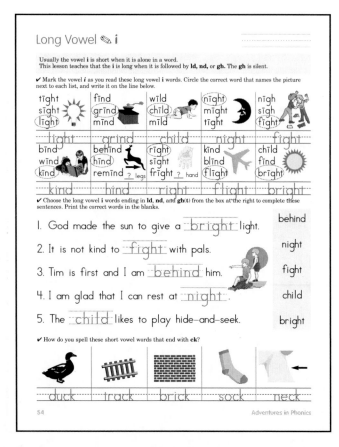

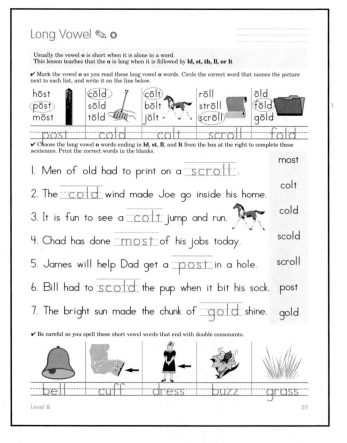

Page 56

Purpose

To teach the sound of **ow** and **ou** as in the words <u>cow</u> and <u>house</u>.

Lesson

If this is the first lesson about the **ow** and **ou** that the student has had, spend as much time as needed for teaching it. Help him read the words from Charts 23 and 24 (page 222 in the workbook), perhaps reading words from Chart 23 for this lesson, and the rest from Chart 24 for the next lesson. Also use the **ow/ou** flashcard.

Listen as the student reads all of the words on the lists and gives the answers to the lesson orally before he completes it independently.

Page 57

Purpose

To teach the sound of **ow** and **ou** as in the words <u>cow</u> and <u>house</u>.

Lesson

Review the sound of **ow** and **ou**. Help the student read the rest of the words that were not read from Chart 24 (page 222 in the workbook). Repetition greatly helps to confirm any lesson. Use drills whenever it is necessary for strengthening reading skills. Also use the **ow/ou** flashcard.

Listen as the student reads all of the words on the lists and gives the answers to the lesson orally before he completes it independently.

Diphthongs ✎ ou and ow

A diphthong is **two** vowel sounds in **one** syllable. The diphthong **ou** makes the sound that is heard in **house**. Another diphthong that makes this sound is **ow** which is used at the end of words as in **cow**, or when words end with **l** as in **owl** or **n** as in **crown**.

✔ Underline the vowels that make the **ou** sound as you read these words with diphthongs. Circle the correct word that names the picture next to each list, and write it on the line below.

how	(owl)	growl	town	house
now	wow	crowd	(down)	proud
(cow)	pow	(vowels)	frown	(mouse)

cow　　owl　　vowels　　down　　mouse

(crown)	tower	bound	sound	count
brown	(flower)	found	(hound)	ounce
gown	power	(round)	pound	(cloud)

crown　　flower　　round　　hound　　cloud

allow	out	mound	ouch	(south)
(clown)	shout	(blouse)	(couch)	scout
plow	(snout)	ground	pouch	mouth

clown　　snout　　blouse　　couch　　south

✔ Choose the words with the diphthongs **ou** or **ow** from the box at the right to complete these sentences. Print the correct words in the blanks.

1. Dry the hound with a brown _towel_.

2. The trail up the _mountain_ is steep.

3. Jed has about a _thousand_ stamps.

4. A bell has a _loud_ sound.

5. At night a light shines on a _fountain_.

thousand
loud
towel
fountain
mountain

56　　Adventures in Phonics

Diphthongs ✎ ou and ow

A diphthong is **two** vowel sounds in **one** syllable. The diphthong **ou** makes the sound that is heard in **house**. Another diphthong that makes this sound is **ow** which is used at the end of words as in **cow**, or when words end with **l** as in **owl** or **n** as in **crown**.

✔ Underline the vowels that make the **ou** sound as you read these words with diphthongs. Circle the correct word that names the picture next to each list, and write it on the line below.

sound	fowl	(hour)	crowd	(sprout)
(scout)	growl	flour	amount	out
pout	(tower)	our	(towel)	doubt

scout　　tower　　hour　　towel　　sprout

✔ Choose the words with the diphthongs **ou** or **ow** from the box at the right to complete these sentences. Print the correct words in the blanks.

1. The brown hound slept on the _ground_.

2. A pig can sniff a sprout with its _snout_.

3. An owl can act like a wise _fowl_.

4. Mother got mad at a mouse in the _house_.

snout
house
fowl
ground

✔ Complete the words by adding the diphthongs. See how quickly you can read the words.

ow			ou
bow	down	thousand	south
how	flower	mountain	ouch
now	crowd	amount	count
plow	chowder	blouse	about
cow	towel	ground	shout

Page 58

Purpose

To teach the sound of **oi** and **oy** as in the words **coin** and **joy**.

Lesson

If this is the first lesson about the **oi** and **oy** that the student has had, spend as much time as needed for teaching it. Help him to read the words from Chart 25 (page 223 in the workbook). Also use the **oi/oy** flashcard.

Listen as the student reads all of the words on the lists and gives the answers to the lesson orally before he completes it independently.

Page 59

Purpose

To review the sound of **oi** and **oy** as in the words **coin** and **joy**.

Lesson

Listen as your student again reads the words from Chart 25 (page 223 in the workbook). Also use the **oi/oy** flashcard.

Prepare for the first part of the lesson by teaching that **oi** is usually followed by another consonant or two, but the **oy** usually is at the end of a word or syllable.

Have the student give the answers to the lesson orally before he completes the page independently.

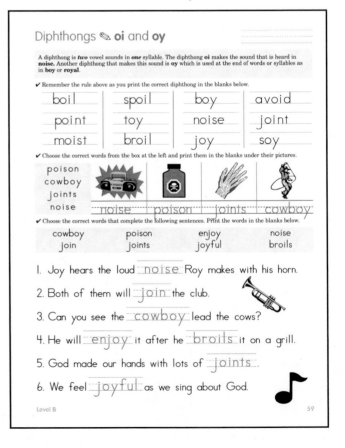

Diphthongs ✎ oi and oy

A diphthong is *two* vowel sounds in *one* syllable. The diphthong **oi** makes the sound that is heard in **noise.** Another diphthong that makes this sound is **oy** which is used at the end of words or syllables as in **boy** or **royal**.

✔ Underline the vowels **oi** and **oy** as you read these words with diphthongs. Circle the correct word that names the picture next to each list, and write it on the line below.

(oil) toil spoil	Roy (toy) joy	join void (coin)	(soil) moist hoist	avoid voice (joints)
oi	toy	coin	soil	joints
(coil) foil broil	enjoy (boy) joys	(royal) foil loyal	Floyd Lloyd (boil)	boil (point) joyful
coil	boy	royal	boil	point

✔ Choose the words with the diphthongs **oi** or **oy** from the box at the right to complete these sentences. Print the correct words in the blanks.

1. Mother will fold __foil__ around Joy's cupcake.
2. It will help to keep it fresh and __moist__.
3. Our class __enjoys__ it when Roy sings.
4. His __voice__ sounds loud and clear.
5. Floyd helps his father dig a hole in the __soil__.
6. He will __hoist__ a flag on a post in the hole.
7. Mother will __broil__ some meat on the grill.

moist
broil
soil
enjoys
foil
voice
hoist

58   Adventures in Phonics

Diphthongs ✎ oi and oy

A diphthong is *two* vowel sounds in *one* syllable. The diphthong **oi** makes the sound that is heard in **noise.** Another diphthong that makes this sound is **oy** which is used at the end of words or syllables as in **boy** or **royal**.

✔ Remember the rule above as you print the correct diphthong in the blanks below.

boil	spoil	boy	avoid
point	toy	noise	joint
moist	broil	joy	soy

✔ Choose the correct words from the box at the left and print them in the blanks under their pictures.

poison cowboy joints noise			
noise	poison	joints	cowboy

✔ Choose the correct words that complete the following sentences. Print the words in the blanks below.

cowboy join	poison joints	enjoy joyful	noise broils

1. Joy hears the loud __noise__ Roy makes with his horn.
2. Both of them will __join__ the club.
3. Can you see the __cowboy__ lead the cows?
4. He will __enjoy__ it after he __broils__ it on a grill.
5. God made our hands with lots of __joints__.
6. We feel __joyful__ as we sing about God.

Level B   59

Page 60

Purpose

To teach the sound of **oo** as in the word <u>zoo</u>.

Lesson

If this is the first lesson about the vowel digraph **oo** that the student has had, spend as much time as needed for teaching it. Help him to read the words from Charts 26 and 27 (page 223 in the workbook). It may be fun if you read one word and your student reads the next word, etc. It is important for him to know the words, so it is worth spending the time. Also use the $\overline{oo}$ flashcard.

Listen as the student reads all of the words on the lists and gives the answers to the lesson orally before he completes it independently.

Page 61

Purpose

To teach the sound of **oo** as in the word **book**.

Lesson

Teach the second sound that the vowel digraph **oo** makes as well as other vowels that make that sound. Spend as much time as necessary. Help your student to read the words found in the first four columns of Chart 28 (page 224 in the workbook). Also use the **oo** flashcard as in **book**.

Emphasize that at times **o**, **u**, and **ou** can also make the sound of **oo** as in **book**. Help him to read the words found on Chart 18 and in the last two columns on chart 28.

Listen as the student reads all of the words on the lists and gives the answers to the lesson orally before he completes it independently.

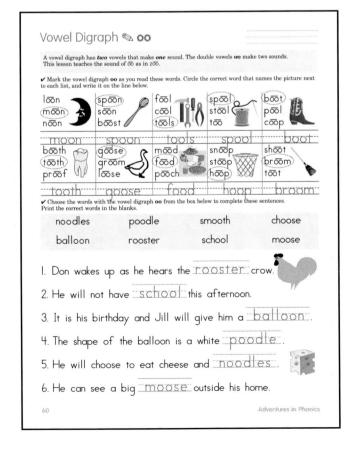

Page 62

Purpose

To teach the sound of **ar** as in the word <u>ark</u>.

Lesson

If this is the first lesson about the **ar** sound that the student has had, spend as much time as needed for teaching it. Help him to read the words from Charts 29 and 30 (page 224 in the workbook). Also use the **är** flashcard.

Listen as the student reads all of the words on the lists and gives the answers to the lesson orally before he completes it independently.

Page 63

Purpose

To teach the sound of **or** as in the word <u>corn</u>.

Lesson

If this is the first lesson about the sound of **or** that the student has had, spend as much time as needed for teaching it. Help him to read the words from Chart 31 (page 225 in the workbook). Also use the **ôr** flashcard.

Listen as the student reads all of the words on the lists and gives the answers to the lesson orally before he completes it independently.

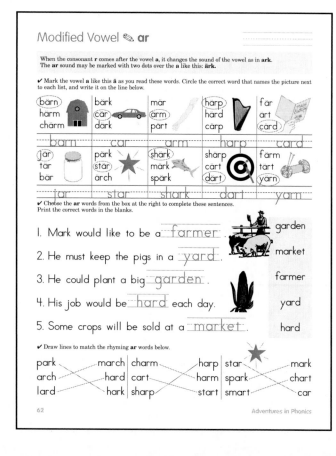

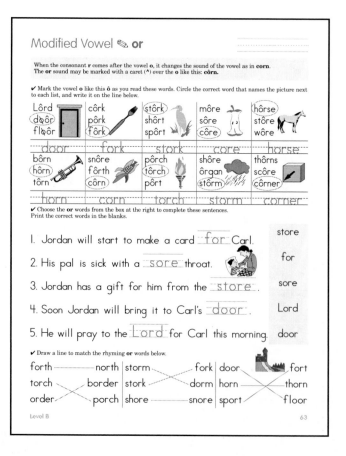

Page 64

Purpose

To teach the sound of **er** as in the words <u>ver</u>se, g<u>ir</u>l, and ch<u>ur</u>ch.

Lesson

Carefully teach this sound with the three sets of letters **er**, **ir**, and **ur**. Help your student to read the words on Chart 32 and the first three columns on Chart 33 (page 225 in the workbook). Also use the **er** flashcard.

Listen as the student reads all of the words on the lists and gives the answers to the lesson orally before he completes it independently.

Page 65

Purpose

To teach the sound of **er** as in the word <u>ear</u>th and (w)<u>or</u>ld.

Lesson

If this is the first lesson about the **er** sound spelled with **ear** and **(w)or** that the student has had, spend as much time as needed for teaching it. Help him to read the words in the last three columns on Chart 33 (page 225 in the workbook). Also use the **er** flashcard.

Listen as the student reads all of the words on the lists and gives the answers to the lesson orally before he completes it independently.

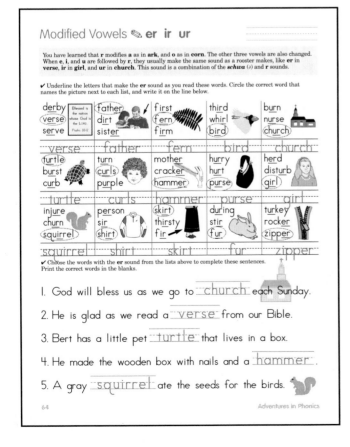

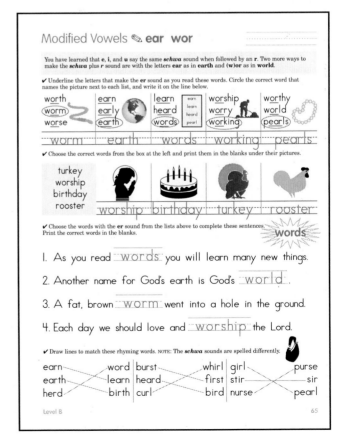

Page 66

Purpose
To teach the sound of **ar** as in the word <u>squ**are**</u>.

Lesson
Carefully teach your student the seven sets of letters that can have the **âr** sound. Help him to read the words from Chart 34 (page 226 in the workbook). Also use the **âr** flashcard; note that the word *their* is also listed on Chart 34 as another spelling for the **âr** sound, but it is not covered in this lesson.

Listen as the student reads all of the words on the lists and gives the answers to the lesson orally before he completes it independently.

Page 67

Purpose
To teach the sound of **ar** as in the word <u>squ**are**</u>.

Lesson
Review the six sets of letters that can have the **âr** sound. Listen as your student again reads the words from Chart 34 (page 226 in the workbook). Also use the **âr** flashcard; note that the word *their* is also listed on Chart 34 as another spelling for the **âr** sound, but it is not covered in this lesson.

Have the student give the answers to the lesson orally before he completes it independently.

Modified Vowels ✎ âr

You have learned the sound of **âr** as in **arm**. These letters may also make the sound of **are** as in **square**. This **ar** sound is marked with a caret (^) over the **a** like this: **squâre**. This sound may also be made as **ar** as in **Mary**, **arr** as in **carrot**, **air** as in **chair**, **err** as in **berry**, **ear** as in **bear**, and **ere** as in **where**.

✔ Underline the **âr** sound as you read these words. Circle the correct word that names the picture next to each list, and write it on the line below.

stare snare (square)	rare carry (carrot)	(hare) fare care	tear wear (bear)	air hair f<u>air</u>
square	**carrot**	**hare**	**bear**	**hair**
(where) dare beware	share spare (stairs)	(error) merry errand	dairy (cherry) declare	bare (pair) air
where	**stairs**	**error**	**cherry**	**pair**
(carry) chair there	blare (chair) berry	(pear) swear dare	marry scary (parrot)	ferry barrel (berry)
carry	**chair**	**pear**	**parrot**	**berry**

✔ Choose the **âr** words from the lists above to complete these sentences. Print the correct words in the blanks.

1. A rabbit may also be called a <u>hare</u>.

2. Barry taught his pet <u>parrot</u> to say some words.

3. I ate a <u>pear</u>, <u>berry</u>, <u>carrot</u>, and <u>cherry</u>.

4. Take care so that the cloth will not <u>tear or wear</u>.

5. The child likes to go up and down the <u>stairs</u>.

Modified Vowels ✎ âr

Review the many ways that you can spell the sound of the **âr** as in **square**: **are** as in **square**, **ar** as in **Mary**, **arr** as in **carrot**, **air** as in **chair**, **err** as in **berry**, **ear** as in **bear**, and **ere** as in **where**.

✔ Choose the correct words from the box at the left and print them in the blanks under their pictures.

marry   chariot   parrot   berry

<u>parrot</u>   <u>marry</u>   <u>chariot</u>   <u>berry</u>

✔ Choose the **âr** words from the list above to complete these sentences. Read the sentences as you print the correct words in the blanks.

1. Ben has a pet <u>parrot</u> that is red and green.

2. Miss Clare can bake <u>berry</u> pies that taste good.

3. In Bible times some men would ride in a <u>chariot</u>.

4. This is a merry affair as Sarah plans to <u>marry</u>.

✔ Choose the letters from the box at the right to answer where you would find the things asked in the questions below. Print the correct letters in the blanks.

1. Where would you find a bear? <u>d</u>   a. to the rabbit

2. Where will Ben and Sarah marry? <u>e</u>   b. to our home

3. Where should we carry the pears? <u>b</u>   c. up and down

4. Where can we go on a stairway? <u>c</u>   d. in the woods

5. Where should this carrot go? <u>a</u>   e. in the church

Page 68

Purpose

To teach the sound of ô as in the words **dog**, **ball**, **saw**, and **haul**.

Lesson

Carefully teach the four sets of letters that can have the ô sound. Help your student to read the words in Chart 35 and the first four lists on Chart 36 (page 226 in the workbook). This may take some time, but patient encouragement will be most beneficial. Also use the ô flashcard.

Listen as the student reads all of the words on the lists and gives the answers to the lesson orally before he completes it independently.

Page 69

Purpose

To continue to teach the sound of ô that is found in the words **daughter** and **bought**.

Lesson

Review the six sets of letters that can make the ô sound. Mention that the letters **gh** are silent in these words.

o   a l   a w

a u   a u g h   o u g h

Listen as he again reads the words from last two columns on Chart 36 (page 226 in the workbook).

Have the student give the answers to the lesson orally before he completes it independently.

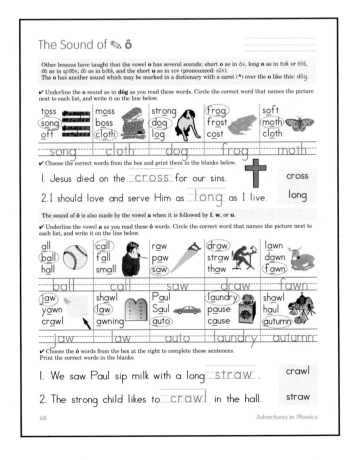

Page 70

Purpose
To review the sounds of **oo, oo, ou, ow, oi,** and **oy.**

Lesson
Print these letters on the board or paper and have your student say them to you.

$\overline{oo}$ $\breve{oo}$ ou   ow   oi   oy

Print these words on the board or paper and ask him to circle one of the above sounds that are in each word. Have him pronounce the word.

moist   tool   enjoy   sound

round   crowd   joint   roost

joy   good   power   shook

You may want to show and discuss the charts of words with these sounds.

Check your student's answers and have him correct any errors as soon as the lesson is completed.

Page 71

Purpose
To review the sounds of **ar, or, er, ir, ur, ear, (w)or.**

Lesson
Print these letters on the board or paper and have your student say them to you.

ar   or   er   ir

ur   ear   (w)or

Print the following words on the board or paper and ask your student to circle one of the above sounds that are in the word. Have him pronounce the word.

hurt   verse   horn   star

bird   word   turn   earn

barn   earth   shirt   corn

Have the student read the list of words orally before he completes the page independently.

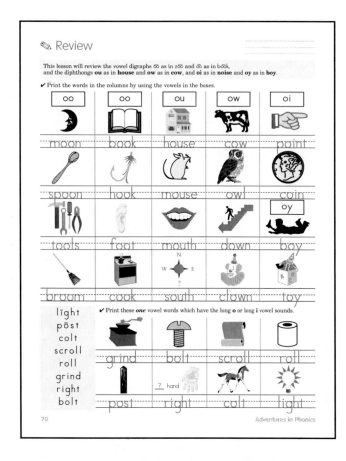

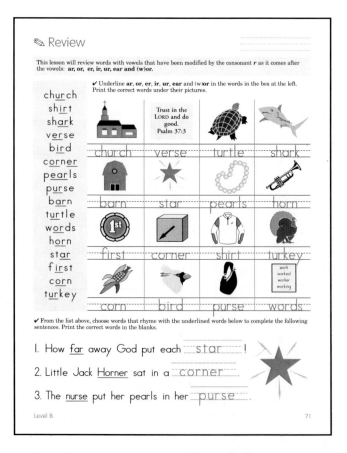

Page 72

Purpose

To review the set of letters that make the sounds of **âr** as in **square** and **ô** as in **dog**.

Lesson

Have your student look at the various ways of spelling the **âr** sound as they are printed on Chart 34 (page 226 in the workbook). Listen to him read the words. It may be best if the work on the top half of the lesson were completed at this time.

Next discuss the sets of letters that are ways of spelling the **ô** sound as they are printed on Charts 35 and 36 (page 226 in the workbook). If you feel the lists would be too much for him to read, it may go better if you read every other word alternately with him.

After you have heard your student read the lesson, have him complete it independently.

Page 73

Purpose

To review the three sounds of **ear**.

Lesson

Print these letters on the board or paper and review the sounds with your student.

$$ēər \qquad ėər \qquad eâr$$

Spend sufficient time reading the first three lines and the list of words on the lesson.

After the page has been completed orally, the student may complete it independently.

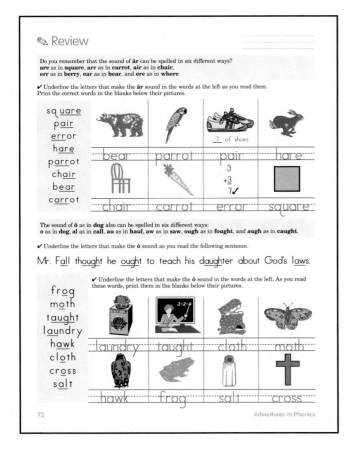

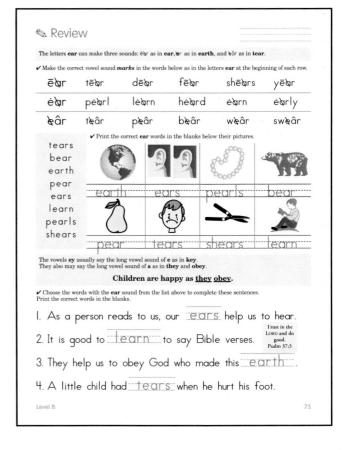

Page 74

Purpose
To teach the soft sound of **c**.

Lesson
Listen to your student read the list of words on Chart 37 (page 227 in the workbook).

When you feel that your student knows the words well, have him complete the answers orally before completing the page independently.

Page 75

Purpose
To teach the soft sound of **g**.

Lesson
Listen to your student read the list of words on Chart 38 (page 227 in the workbook).

When you feel that he knows the words well, have your student complete the answers orally before completing the page independently.

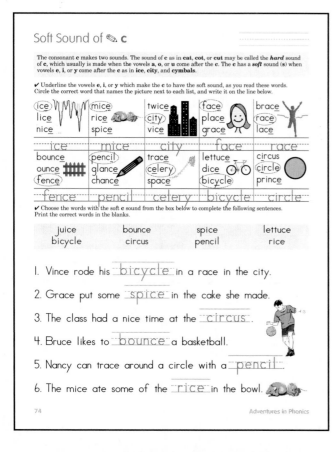

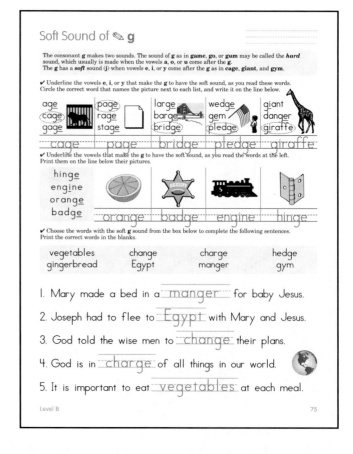

Page 76

Purpose

To teach the consonant digraphs **kn** and **wr**.

Lesson

After you have discussed these digraphs with your student, have him read the words in the first five columns on Chart 42 (page 228 in the workbook) until he can say them quickly. Also use the **kn** and **wr** flashcards.

After you have heard your student read the lesson, have him complete it independently.

Page 77

Purpose

To teach the sounds of sets of letters with silent consonants.

Lesson

Study the sets of sounds at the top of the page on the lesson. Spend as much time as necessary to listen to your student work his way through the entire lesson orally. Encourage him to do his work carefully.

When you feel that he knows the words well, have your student complete the answers orally before completing the page independently.

Silent Consonants ✎ kn wr

The **k** is silent when it is followed by **n** as in knot and knee.
The **w** is silent when it is followed by **r** as in write and wrap.

✔ Cross out the silent **k** as you read these words. Print the correct words on the line below their pictures.

kneel
knife
knot
knit

knot   knit   kneel   knife

✔ Cross out the silent **k** in the words at the left. Print the correct words in the blanks below.

knuckles
know
knot
knew

1. Ken knew how to tie a knot.

2. Kay hit her knuckles on the wall.

3. Do you know how to read the Bible?

✔ Cross out the silent **w** in the words in the box below. Print the underlined words under their pictures.
Choose from these words to complete the following sentences. Print the correct words on the blanks below.

| Wrestle | Wrench | Wreck | Wrong | Wrinkle |
| Wreath | Wrap | Wren | Wrist | Write |

4
+5
7 ✓

wrong   wreath   write   wrench   wren

1. If we wring out the wet shirt it will wrinkle.

2. Ron will wrap a cloth around his sore wrist.

3. The boys do not have wrath as they wrestle.

76   Adventures in Phonics

✎ Silent Consonants

There are several other sets of letters in which one consonant or vowel may be silent, such as:
gn as in gnaw, **mb** as in lamb, **bt** as in doubt, **gu** as in guess, **bu** as in build, and **mn** as in hymn.

✔ Cross out the silent letter in each word. Print the correct words that name the pictures below.

| thumb | gnat | build | hymn | lamb |

hymn   lamb   thumb   gnat   build

✔ Choose the correct words from the box at the left and print them in the blanks below.

guards
climb
tomb

1. Jesus came out from the tomb.

2. The guards became as dead men.

3. I will need a guide if I climb a mountain.

✔ Answer these questions by printing **yes** or **no**.

1. Can a gnat tie a knot? no

2. Do you know how to write your name? yes

3. Would a wrench help a man build a bridge? yes

4. Does a wren know how to wrap a gift? no

5. Would you like to pet a soft little lamb? yes

6. Should children know how to obey their parents? yes

Level B   77

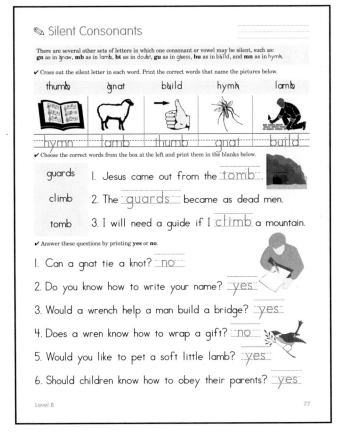

Page 78

Purpose
To teach the short vowel **e** sound of **ea**.

Lesson
Listen to your student read the list of words on Chart 39 (page 227 in the workbook). Discuss words that rhyme, mentioning that words must have the same vowel sounds and ending sounds. Say these words to train him to hear the matching vowel sounds:

care	rare	night	fight
lace	face	dead	head
raw	thaw	stool	pool

When you feel that he knows the words well, have your student complete the answers orally before completing the page independently.

Page 79

Purpose
To teach the long vowel **a** sound of **ea** and the long vowel **u** sound of **ou** as in **you**.

Lesson
Listen to your student read the first list of words on Chart 40 (page 228 in the workbook). Discuss all of the sounds **ea** can make:

ēb—ear   ĕb—head   bā—steak

Mention that when the consonant **r** follows **ea**, it makes several more sounds. It may be best to complete the top section of the lesson at this time.

Discuss the directions for the middle section, teaching that the **ou** sometimes has the long **u** as in **you** and **through**. When he can read the **ou** words quickly, have your student print the words in the blanks under the correct picture.

Does he understand about rhyming words? Discuss again that the vowel sounds and endings must match in rhyming words.

tame	same	soup	loop
note	goat	weep	keep
hook	took	steak	wake

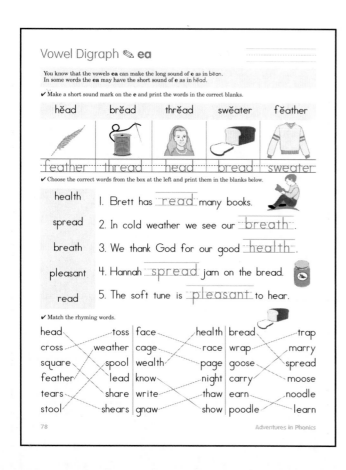

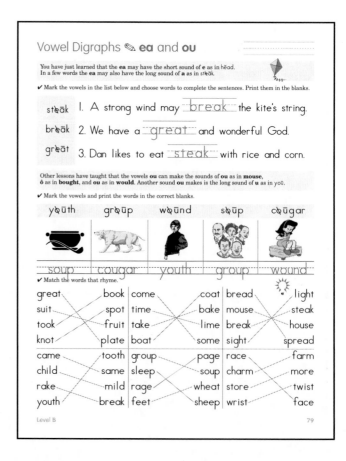

Page 80

Purpose
To teach about compound words.

Lesson
Explain how two special words are put together to form one (**compound**) word as in:

mailbox doorway snowman

sailboat bluebird pancake

This lesson introduces the student to *simple word division*; that is, the divison of compound words. Have your student divide the words above, as follows:

mail-box door-way snow-man

sail-boat blue-bird pan-cake

Dividing words by syllables will be introduced later.

Go through the lesson and have the student give the answers orally before completing it independently.

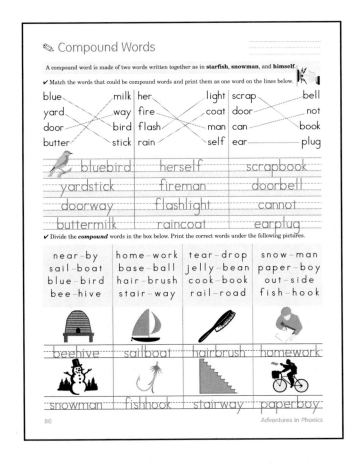

Page 81

Purpose
To review about compound words.

Lesson
Review how two special words are put together to form one (**compound**) word as in:

rosebud teapot highway

notebook starfish airport

This lesson also emphasizes *simple word division*; that is, the divison of compound words. Have your student divide the words above, as follows:

rose-bud tea-pot high-way

note-book star-fish air-port

Discuss the lesson and have the student give the answers orally before completing it independently.

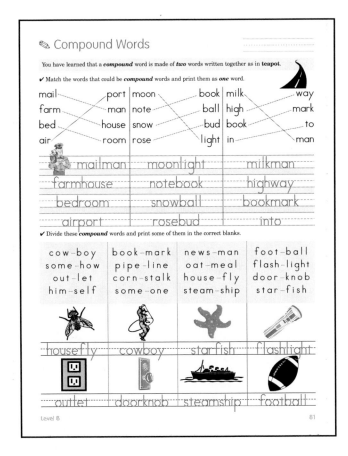

Page 82

Purpose

To review words that are spelled with the short vowel sound of **a**.

Lesson

Listen to your student read the words in Chart 1 (page 215 in the workbook).

If he has no difficulty and can quickly say the words, discuss the lesson and have him answer orally before he completes it independently.

Page 83

Purpose

To review more words that are spelled with the short vowel sound of **a**.

Lesson

Listen to your student read the words in Chart 2 (page 215 in the workbook).

If he has no difficulty and can quickly say the words, discuss the lesson and have him answer orally before he completes it independently.

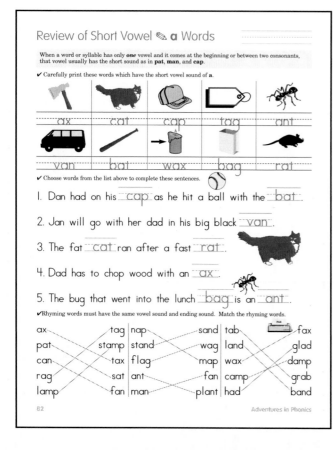

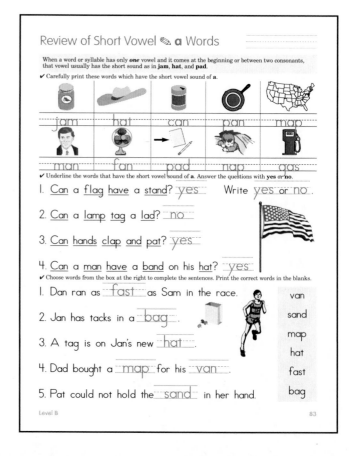

Page 84

Purpose
To review words that are spelled with the short vowel sound of **e**.

Lesson
Listen to your student read the words in Chart 3 (page 215 in the workbook).

If he has no difficulty and can quickly say the words, discuss the lesson and have him answer orally before he completes it independently.

Page 85

Purpose
To review more words that are spelled with the short vowel sound of **e**.

Lesson
Listen to your student read the words in Chart 3.

If he has no difficulty and can quickly say the words, discuss the lesson and have him answer orally before he completes it independently.

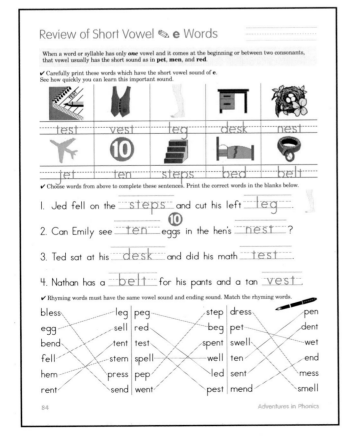

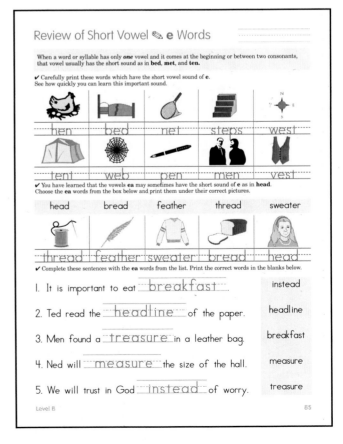

Page 86

Purpose
To review words that are spelled with the short vowel sound of **i**.

Lesson
Listen to your student read the words in Chart 4 (page 216 in the workbook).

If he has no difficulty and can quickly say the words, discuss the lesson and have him answer orally before he completes it independently.

Page 87

Purpose
To review more words that are spelled with the short vowel sound of **i**.

Lesson
Listen to your student read the words in Chart 4.

If he has no difficulty and can quickly say the words, discuss the lesson and have him answer orally before he completes it independently.

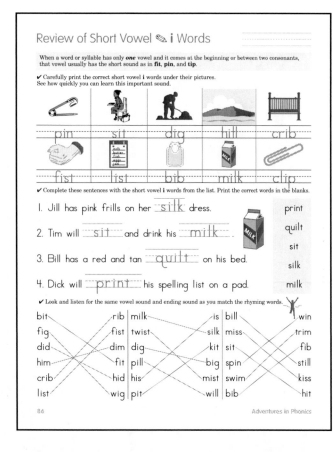

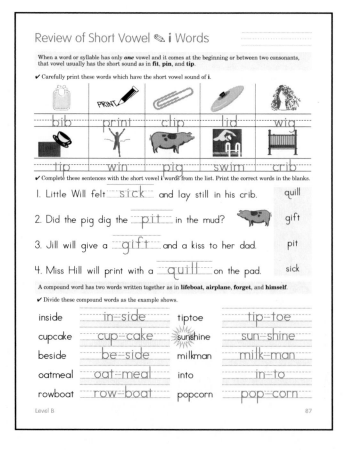

Page 88

Purpose
To review words that are spelled with the short vowel sound of **o**.

Lesson
Listen to your student read the words in Chart 5 (page 216 in the workbook).

If he has no difficulty and can quickly say the words, discuss the lesson and have him answer orally before he completes it independently.

Page 89

Purpose
To review more words that are spelled with the short vowel sound of **o**.

Lesson
Listen to your student read the words in Chart 5.

If he has no difficulty and can quickly say the words, discuss the lesson and have him answer orally before he completes it independently.

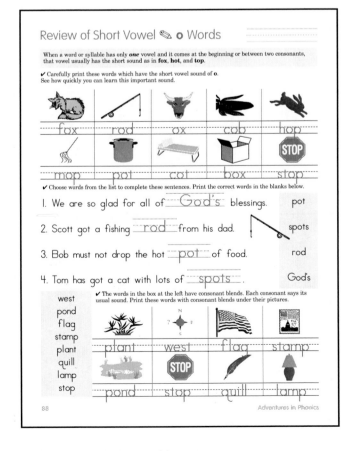

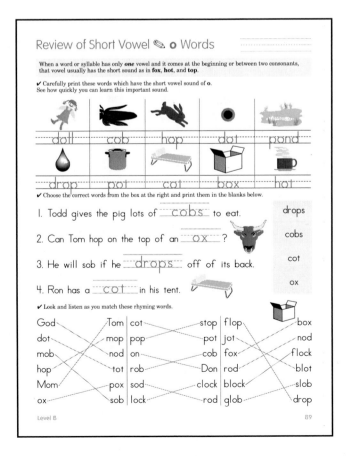

Page 90

Purpose
To review words that are spelled with the short vowel sound of **u**.

Lesson
Listen to your student read the words in Chart 6 (page 216 in the workbook).

If he has no difficulty and can quickly say the words, discuss the lesson and have him answer orally before he completes it independently.

Page 91

Purpose
To review more words that are spelled with the short vowel sound of **u**.

Lesson
Listen to your student read the words in Chart 6. Also have him read Chart 18 (page 220 in the workbook).

If he has no difficulty and can quickly say the words, discuss the lesson and have him answer orally before he completes it independently.

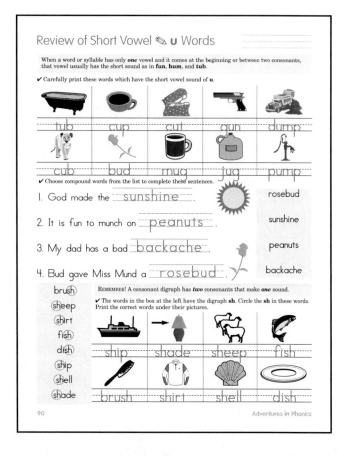

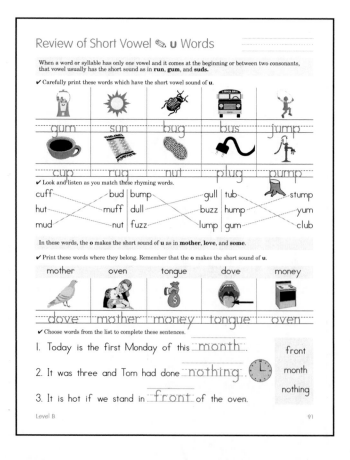

Page 92

Purpose

To review words that are spelled with *double* consonants **ss**, **ff**, **ll**, and **zz**.

Lesson

Look over Charts 2, 3, 4 and 6 (pages 215 and 216 in the workbook) with your student and have him find and read the words that end with these double letters.

If he has no difficulty and can quickly say the words, discuss the lesson and have him answer orally before he completes it independently.

Note: The word *bitt* appears in the first matching list in the middle of page 92; it means "a post or pair of posts fixed on the deck of a ship for securing lines."

Page 93

Purpose

To review short vowel words that end with **ck**.

Lesson

Listen to your student read the words on Chart 7 (page 217 in the workbook).

If he has no difficulty and can quickly say the words, discuss the lesson and have him answer orally before he completes it independently.

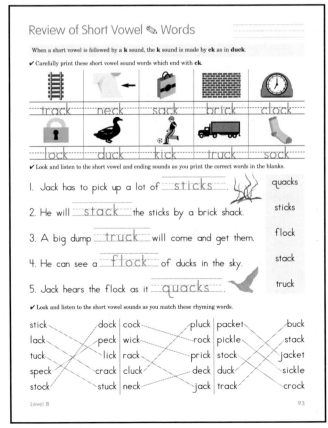

Page 94

Purpose

To review words that are spelled with the long vowel sound of **a**.

Lesson

Listen to your student read the words in Chart 10 (page 218 in the workbook).

If he has no difficulty and can quickly say the words, discuss the lesson and have him answer orally before he completes it independently.

Page 95

Purpose

To review more words that are spelled with the long vowel sound of **a**.

Lesson

Listen to your student read the words in Chart 11 (page 218 in the workbook).

If he has no difficulty and can quickly say the words, discuss the lesson and have him answer orally before he completes it independently.

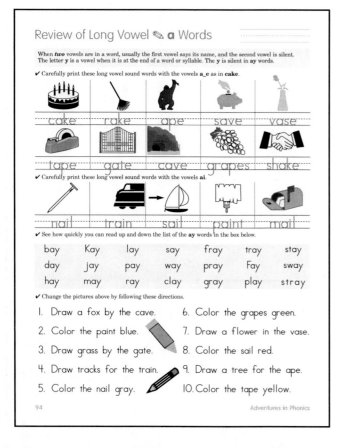

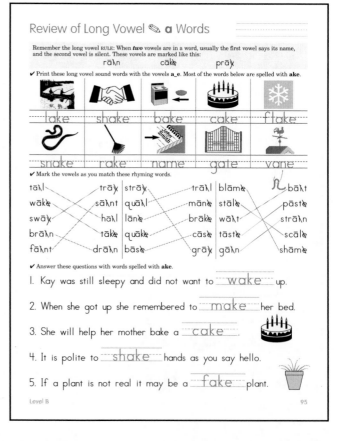

Page 96

Purpose

To review words that are spelled with the long vowel sound of **e**.

Lesson

Listen to your student read the words in Chart 12 (page 218 in the workbook).

If he has no difficulty and can quickly say the words, discuss the lesson and have him answer orally before he completes it independently.

Page 97

Purpose

To review more words that are spelled with the long vowel sound of **e**. To review a few words with the consonant digraph **ch**.

Lesson

Listen to your student read the words in Chart 13 (page 219 in the workbook).

If he has no difficulty and can quickly say the words, discuss the lesson and have him answer orally before he completes it independently.

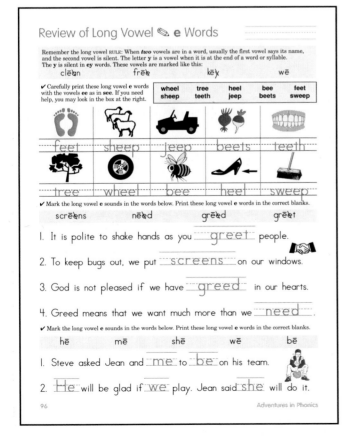

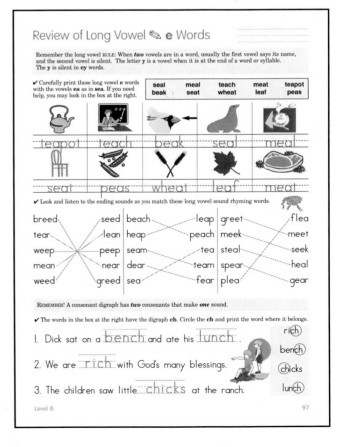

Page 98

Purpose
To review words that are spelled with the long vowel sound of **i**.

Lesson
Listen to your student read the words in Chart 14 (page 219 in the workbook).

If he has no difficulty and can quickly say the words, discuss the lesson and have him answer orally before he completes it independently.

Page 99

Purpose
To review more words that are spelled with the long vowel sound of **i**.

Lesson
Listen to your student read the words in Chart 15 (page 219 in the workbook). Also review the words in Chart 21 (page 221 in the workbook).

If he has no difficulty and can quickly say the words, discuss the lesson and have him answer orally before he completes it independently.

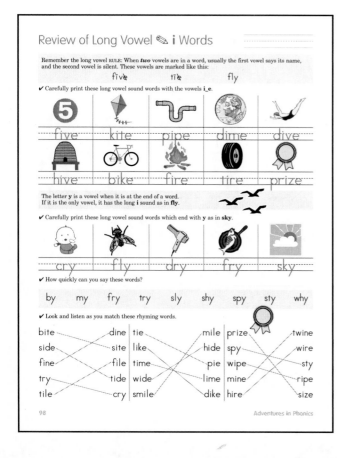

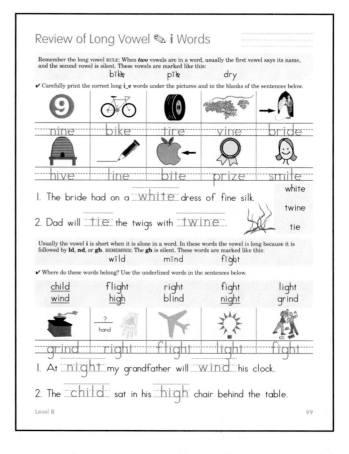

Page 100

Purpose

To review words that are spelled with the long vowel sound of **o**.

Lesson

Listen to your student read the words in Chart 16 (page 220 in the workbook).

If the student has no difficulty and can quickly say the words, discuss the lesson and have him answer orally before he completes it independently.

Page 101

Purpose

To review more words that are spelled with the long vowel sound of **o**.

Lesson

Listen to your student read the words in Chart 17 (page 220 in the workbook). Also have him read the words in Chart 22 (page 222 in the workbook).

If the student has no difficulty and can quickly say the words, discuss the lesson and have him answer orally before he completes it independently.

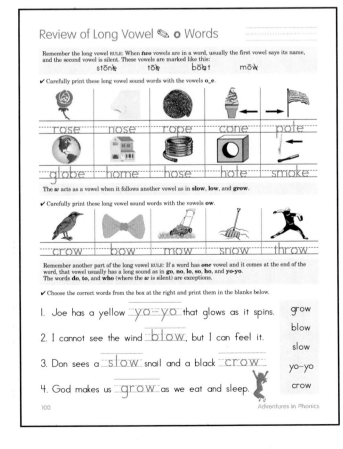

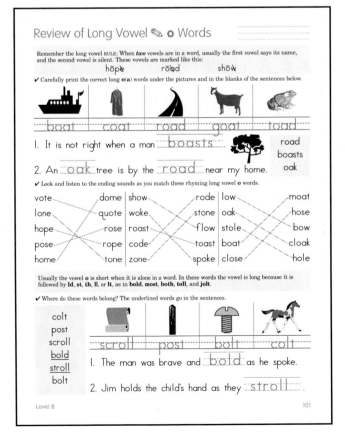

Page 102

Purpose

To review words that are spelled with the long vowel sound of **u**.

Lesson

Listen to your student read the words in Chart 19 (page 221 in the workbook).

If the student has no difficulty and can quickly say the words, discuss the lesson and have him answer orally before he completes it independently.

Page 103

Purpose

To review words that have the long **u** sound and are spelled with **oo**.

Lesson

Listen to your student read the words in Chart 26 (page 223 in the workbook).

If the student has no difficulty and can quickly say the words, discuss the lesson and have him answer orally before he completes it independently.

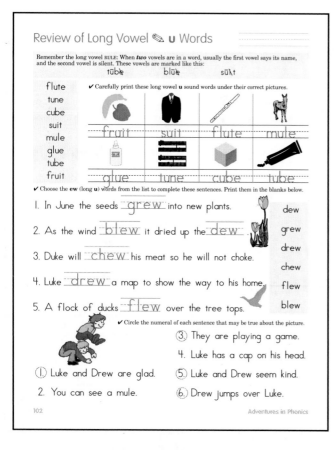

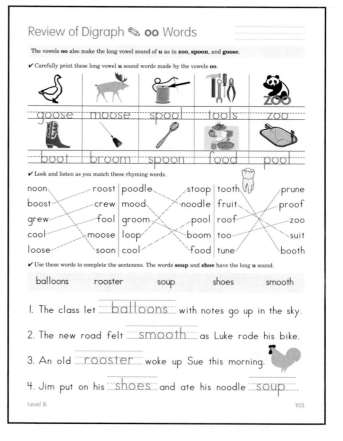

Page 104

Purpose

To review words that are spelled with the sound of **oo** as in **zoo** and **oo** as in **book**.

Lesson

Listen to your student read the words in Chart 27 (page 223 in the workbook) and the first four columns in Chart 28 (page 224 in the workbook).

If the student has no difficulty and can quickly say the words, discuss the lesson and have him answer orally before he completes it independently.

Page 105

Purpose

To review words that are spelled with the sound of **oo** as in **zoo** and **oo** as in **book**.

Lesson

Listen to your student read the words in the last two columns of Chart 28.

If the student has no difficulty and can quickly say the words, discuss the lesson and have him answer orally before he completes it independently.

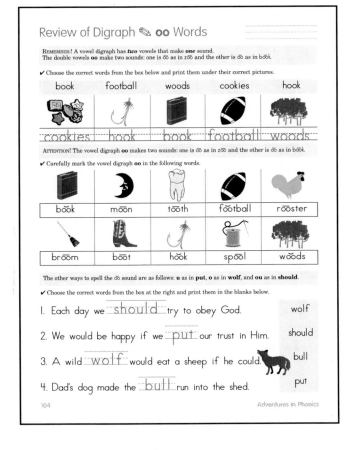

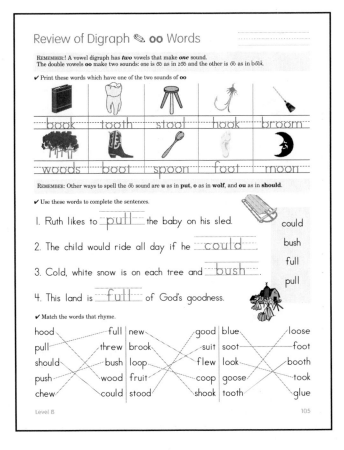

Page 106

Purpose

1. To recall that a *diphthong* is two vowels sounded so that both vowels can be heard blended together as one.

2. To review words that have the diphthong sound of **ou** made by two sets of vowels: **ow** as in **cow** and **ou** as in **house**. Remember that in some words the **ow** has the long **o** sound.

Lesson

Listen to your student read the words in Chart 23 (page 222 in the workbook).

If the student has no difficulty and can quickly say the words, discuss the lesson and have him answer orally before he completes it independently.

Page 107

Purpose

To review words that have the diphthong sound of **ou** made by two sets of vowels: **ow** as in **cow** and **ou** as in **house**. Remember that in some words the **ow** has the long **o** sound.

Lesson

Listen to your student read the words in Chart 24 (page 222 in the workbook).

If the student has no difficulty and can quickly say the words, discuss the lesson and have him answer orally before he completes it independently.

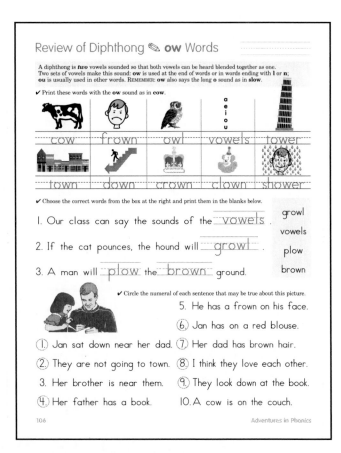

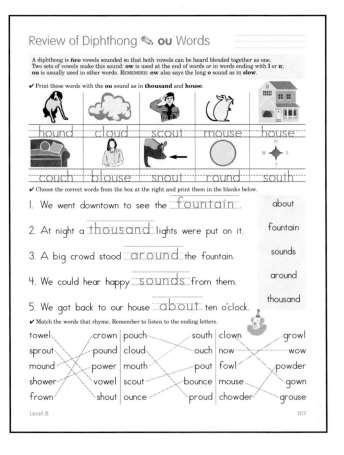

Page 108

Purpose

1. To review words that have the diphthong sound of **oi** made by two sets of vowels: **oi** as in **noise** and **oy** as in **boy**.

2. To review the two sounds made by the consonant digraph **th**.

Lesson

Listen to your student read the words in Chart 25 (page 223 in the workbook), as well as the **th** words in Chart 9 (page 217 in the workbook).

If the student has no difficulty and can quickly say the words, discuss the lesson and have him answer orally before he completes it independently.

Note that the matching exercise at the top of the page may have these alternate answers: *royal* and *spoil* may be matched, and *coil* and *loyal* may also be matched. However, the preferred matches are *royal* and *loyal*, and *coil* and *spoil*.

Page 109

Purpose

1. To review words that have the diphthong sound of **oi** made by two sets of vowels: **oi** as in **noise** and **oy** as in **boy**.

2. To review the two sounds made by the consonant digraph **th**.

Lesson

Listen to your student read the words in Chart 25.

If the student has no difficulty and can quickly say the words, discuss the lesson and have him answer orally before he completes it independently.

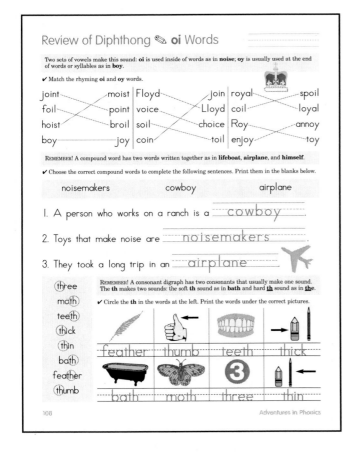

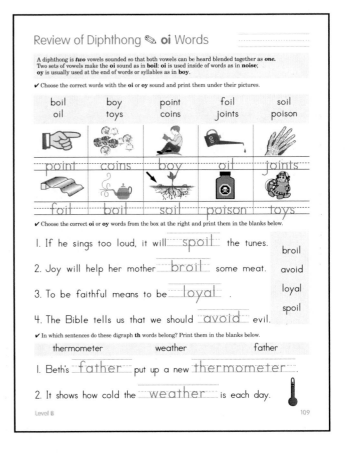

Page 110

Purpose

To review words that have the sound of **är**.

Lesson

Listen to your student read the words in Chart 29 (page 224 in the workbook).

If the student has no difficulty and can quickly say the words, discuss the lesson and have him answer orally before he completes it independently.

Page 111

Purpose

1. To review words that have the sound of **är**.

2. To discuss the importance of suffixes.

Lesson

Listen to your student read the words in Chart 30 (page 224 in the workbook).

If the student has no difficulty and can quickly say the words, discuss the lesson and have him answer orally before he completes it independently.

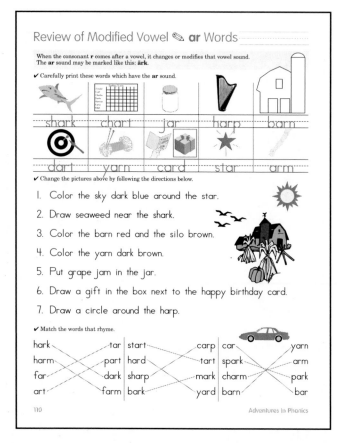

<table>
<tr><td>

Page 112

Purpose

1. To review words that have the sound of **ôr**.

2. To discuss compound words.

Lesson

Listen to your student read the words in Chart 31 (page 225 in the workbook).

If the student has no difficulty and can quickly say the words, discuss the lesson and have him answer orally before he completes it independently.

</td><td>

Page 113

Purpose

1. To review words that have the sound of **ôr**.

2. To discuss the suffix **ness**.

Lesson

Listen to your student read the words in Chart 31.

If the student has no difficulty and can quickly say the words, discuss the lesson and have him answer orally before he completes it independently.

</td></tr>
</table>

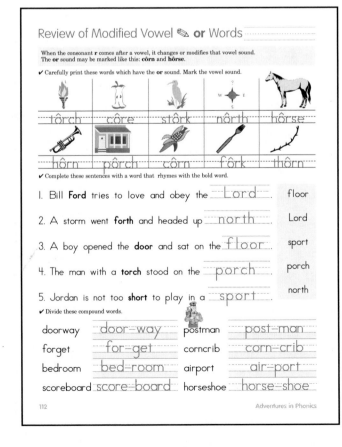

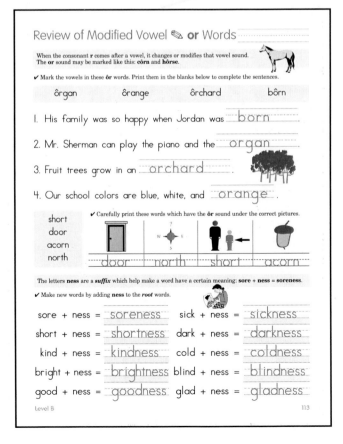

Page 114

Purpose
To review words that have the sound of **ûr** made by **er**, **ir**, and **ur**.

Lesson
Listen to your student read the **er** and **ir** words in Chart 32 and the **ur** words in Chart 33 (page 225 in the workbook).

If the student has no difficulty and can quickly say the words, discuss the lesson and have him answer orally before he completes it independently.

Page 115

Purpose
1. To review words that have the sound of **ûr** made by **ear** and **(w)or**.

2. To review the suffix **er**.

Lesson
Listen as your student reads the words in Chart 33 (page 225 in the workbook) that are spelled with the letters **ear** and **(w)or**.

If the student has no difficulty and can quickly say the words, discuss the lesson and have him answer orally before he completes it independently.

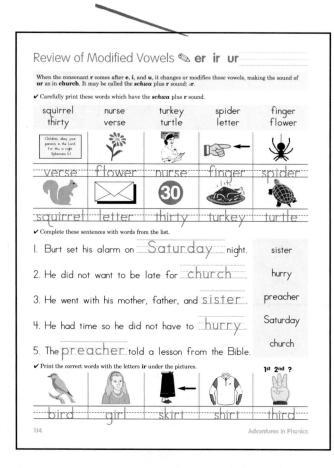

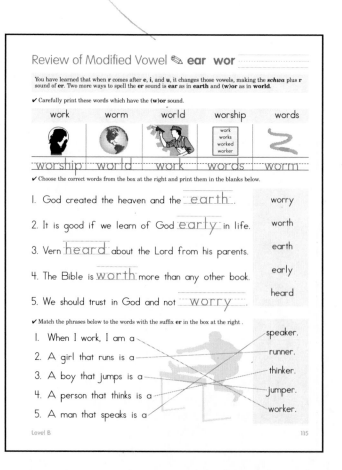

Page 116

Purpose

To review words that have the sound of **âr** as in **are**, **arr**, **air**, **err**, and **ear**.

Lesson

Listen as your student reads the words in Chart 34 (page 226 in the workbook).

If the student has no difficulty and can quickly say the words, discuss the lesson and have him answer orally before he completes it independently.

Page 117

Purpose

To review words that have the sound of **âr** as in **are**, **arr**, **air**, **err**, **ear**, **ere**, and **eir**.

Lesson

If your student can read the words in Chart 34 quickly, you may not feel it necessary to have him read it again.

Discuss the lesson and have your student answer orally before he does the work independently.

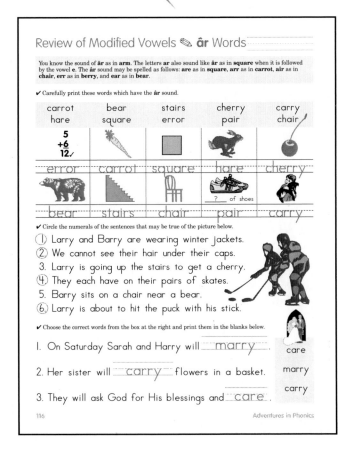

Review of Modified Vowels ✎ **âr** Words

You know the sound of **är** as in **arm**. The letters **ar** also sound like **âr** as in **square** when it is followed by the vowel **e**. The **âr** sound may be spelled as follows: **are** as in **square**, **arr** as in **carrot**, **air** as in **chair**, **err** as in **berry**, and **ear** as in **bear**.

✔ Carefully print these words which have the **âr** sound.

carrot	bear	stairs	cherry	carry
hare	square	error	pair	chair

| 5 +6 12✓ | | | | |

error | carrot | square | hare | cherry
bear | stairs | chair | pair | carry

✔ Circle the numerals of the sentences that may be true of the picture below.

① Larry and Barry are wearing winter jackets.
② We cannot see their hair under their caps.
3. Larry is going up the stairs to get a cherry.
④ They each have on their pairs of skates.
5. Barry sits on a chair near a bear.
⑥ Larry is about to hit the puck with his stick.

✔ Choose the correct words from the box at the right and print them in the blanks below.

I. On Saturday Sarah and Harry will   marry .

2. Her sister will   carry   flowers in a basket.

3. They will ask God for His blessings and   care .

care
marry
carry

116   Adventures in Phonics

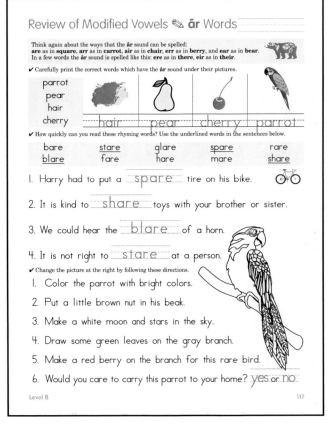

Review of Modified Vowels ✎ **âr** Words

Think again about the ways that the **âr** sound can be spelled:
are as in **square**, **arr** as in **carrot**, **air** as in **chair**, **err** as in **berry**, and **ear** as in **bear**.
In a few words the **âr** sound is spelled like this: **ere** as in **there**, **eir** as in **their**.

✔ Carefully print the correct words which have the **âr** sound under their pictures.

parrot				
pear				
hair				
cherry	hair	pear	cherry	parrot

✔ How quickly can you read these rhyming words? Use the underlined words in the sentences below.

bare	stare	glare	spare	rare
blare	fare	hare	mare	share

I. Harry had to put a   spare   tire on his bike.

2. It is kind to   share   toys with your brother or sister.

3. We could hear the   blare   of a horn.

4. It is not right to   stare   at a person.

✔ Change the picture at the right by following these directions.

I. Color the parrot with bright colors.

2. Put a little brown nut in his beak.

3. Make a white moon and stars in the sky.

4. Draw some green leaves on the gray branch.

5. Make a red berry on the branch for this rare bird.

6. Would you care to carry this parrot to your home? yes or no

Level B   117

Page 118

Purpose

To review words that have the sound of ô as in **dog**, **ball**, **auto**, and **paw**.

Lesson

Listen as your student reads the words in Chart 35 and the first four columns in Chart 36 (page 226 in the workbook).

If the student has no difficulty and can quickly say the words, discuss the lesson and have him answer orally before he completes it independently.

Page 119

Purpose

To review words that have the sound of ô as in **daughter** and **bought**.

Lesson

Listen as your student reads the last two columns of words in Chart 36.

If the student has no difficulty and can quickly say the words, discuss the lesson and have him answer orally before he completes it independently.

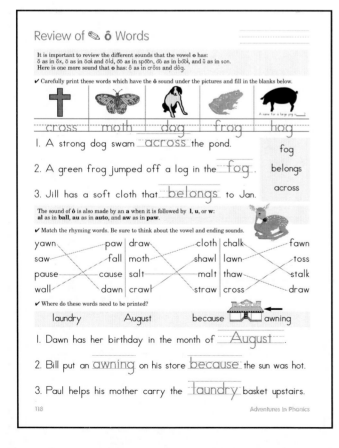

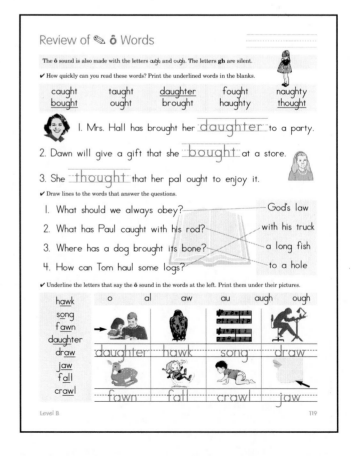

Page 120

Purpose
To review words that have the soft sound of **c** as in **ice**, **city**, and **cymbals**.

Lesson
Review the rule which teaches that the **c** usually has the sound of **s** when it is followed by the vowels **e**, **i**, or **y**. The letter **k** makes the hard sound in the words with these vowels, as in **kite**, **cake**, and **hanky**.

Listen as your student reads the words in Chart 37 (page 227 in the workbook).

If the student has no difficulty and can quickly say the words, discuss the lesson and have him answer orally before he completes it independently.

Page 121

Purpose
To review words that have the soft sound of **g** as in **cage**, **giant**, and **gym**.

Lesson
Review the rule which teaches that the **g** usually has the sound of **j** when it is followed by vowels **e**, **i**, or **y**. There are a few exceptions such as: **get** and **gift**.

Listen as your student reads the words in Chart 38 (page 227 in the workbook).

If the student has no difficulty and can quickly say the words, discuss the lesson and have him answer orally before he completes it independently.

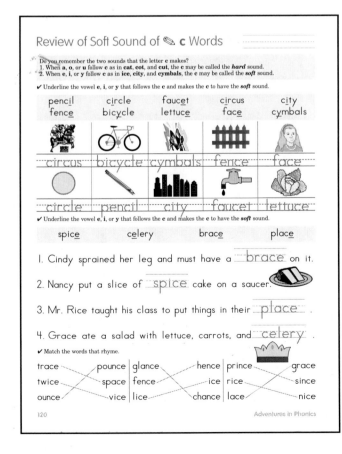

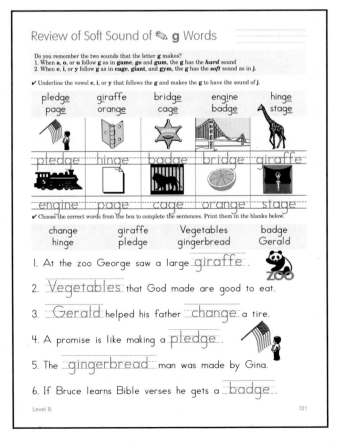

Page 122

Purpose

To review words with the digraphs **sh** and **wh**.

Lesson

Listen as your student reads the **sh** and **wh** words in Charts 8 and 9 (page 217 in the workbook).

If the student has no difficulty and can quickly say the words, discuss the lesson and have him answer orally before he completes it independently.

Page 123

Purpose

To review words with the digraphs **kn** and **wr**.

Lesson

Listen as your student reads the **kn** and **wr** words in Chart 42 (page 228 in the workbook).

If the student has no difficulty and can quickly say the words, discuss the lesson and have him answer orally before he completes it independently.

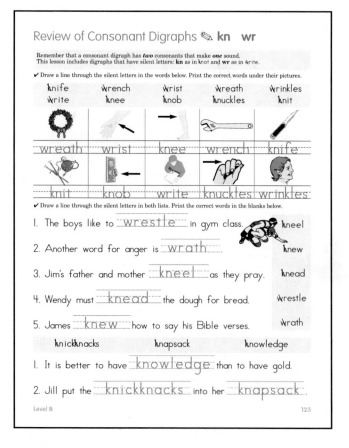

Page 124

Purpose
To review words with silent letters.

Lesson
Carefully and thoroughly discuss the lesson with your student and have him answer orally before he completes it independently.

Page 125

Purpose
To review words with silent letters such as:

calf   walk   watch   calm

It is interesting that the silent letters follow the vowel **a**.

Lesson
Carefully and thoroughly discuss the lesson with your student and have him answer orally before he completes it independently.

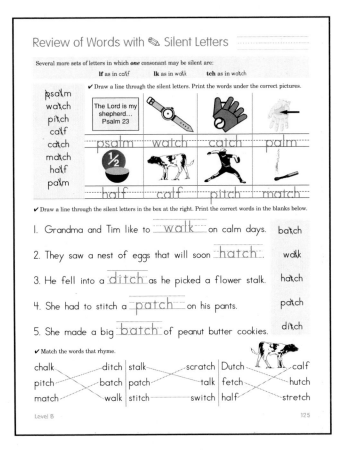

Review of Words with ✎ Silent Letters

Several sets of letters in which **one** consonant or vowel may be silent are:
gn as in gnow   **mb** as in lamb   **bt** as in doubt
gu as in guess   **mn** as in hymn   **bu** as in build
There are only a few words with these sets of silent letters.

lamb
thumb
building
climb
guards
hymn
gnat
gnu

✔ Cross out the silent letter in each word and carefully print the answers.

gnu   climb   hymn   building

lamb   guards   thumb   gnat

✔ Choose words from the list above to complete these sentences.

1. A large animal that you may see in Africa is a gnu.

2. Tom enjoys seeing men build a building.

3. The shepherd will climb down a cliff to get the lamb.

4. Rachel likes to sing a hymn as she helps her mother.

5. The guards stood near the castle as they guarded.

✔ Complete these sentences with the correct words in the box to the right.

1. Jesus came out of the tomb and lives in heaven.

2. We need Him to guide us as our shepherd.

guide
tomb

124   Adventures in Phonics

Review of Words with ✎ Silent Letters

Several more sets of letters in which **one** consonant may be silent are:

lf as in calf   **lk** as in walk   **tch** as in watch

psalm
watch
pitch
calf
catch
match
half
palm

✔ Draw a line through the silent letters. Print the words under the correct pictures.

The Lord is my shepherd... Psalm 23

psalm   watch   catch   palm

half   calf   pitch   match

✔ Draw a line through the silent letters in the box at the right. Print the correct words in the blanks below.

1. Grandma and Tim like to walk on calm days.

2. They saw a nest of eggs that will soon hatch.

3. He fell into a ditch as he picked a flower stalk.

4. She had to stitch a patch on his pants.

5. She made a big batch of peanut butter cookies.

batch
walk
hatch
patch
ditch

✔ Match the words that rhyme.

chalk   ditch   stalk   scratch Dutch   calf
pitch   batch   patch   talk   fetch   hutch
match   walk   stitch   switch   half   stretch

Level B   125

Page 126

Purpose

To review words with the letters **ng** and **nk**.

Lesson

Have your student read these lists of words.

bang	bring	sling	gong
gang	ding	swing	long
hang	fling	spring	wrong
rang	ring	thing	song
sang	sing	wing	thong

bank	rank	ink	rink
blank	sank	blink	sink
crank	tank	drink	think
drank	thank	pink	wink

Listen as your student reads the **ng** and **nk** words in Chart 41 (page 228 in the workbook).

Carefully and thoroughly discuss the lesson and have your student answer orally before he completes it independently.

Page 127

Purpose

To review words with the letters **ea** and **ou**.

Lesson

Chart 40 (page 228 in the workbook) has the three most commonly used words with **ea** having the long sound of **a**. Review the three sounds made by **ea**, and listen as these columns are read by your student.

ēā	ĕă	ēă
break	bread	ear
steak	thread	heat
great	feather	meal

Have your student read these long **u** words.

you	soup	through
group	wound	youth

Carefully discuss the lesson and have your student answer orally before he completes the work independently.

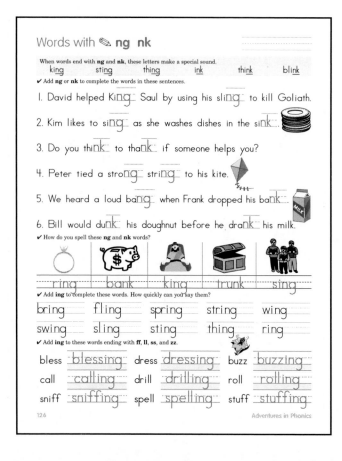

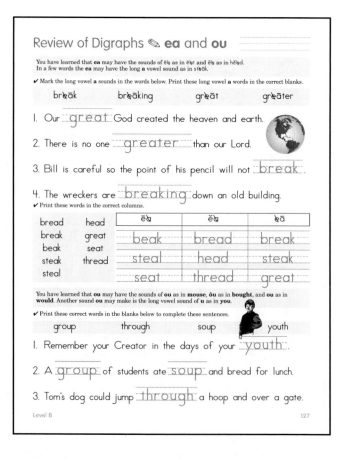

Page 128

Purpose
To work with words that have the vowel **a** making the short sound of **u**. This is called a *schwa* sound and may be made by any of the vowels.

ago   around

Lesson
Carefully discuss the lesson and have your student answer orally before he completes the work independently.

Page 129

Purpose
1. To teach the proper use of **a** and **an** before nouns.

2. Review words with the soft sounds of **c** and **g**.

Lesson
Remind the student about the vowels **a e i o u**.

Explain that when a word begins with a vowel, we may use the word **an** before that word as in:

an ant | an apple | an egg

an oar | an owl | an idea

an inch | an eel | an eagle

If a word begins with a consonant, we would use just the letter **a**, as in:

a book | a car | a piano

a door | a melon | a race

Think about what kind of a letter is at the beginning of each word—a consonant or a vowel.

Discuss the lesson and have your student answer orally before he completes the work independently.

Schwa Sound of ✎ a

Remember that the vowel **o** may have the short vowel **u** sound as in these words:

mother   shovel   from   color   wonder   love   Monday   nothing   of

Each of the vowels may make the short sound of **u**. A dictionary may show a symbol like this ə for that sound which is called a *schwa* sound. Some words begin with the letter a having this sound as in arose.

✔ Read these words and then divide them as you print them.

alike — a-like   ago — a-go   alive — a-live

awake — a-wake   asleep — a-sleep   awhile — a-while

afraid — a-fraid   about — a-bout   ahead — a-head

away — a-way   avoid — a-void   astray — a-stray

apart — a-part   arose — a-rose   aloud — a-loud

✔ Use the underlined words above to complete these sentences. Print them in the blanks below.

1. Long **ago** Jesus died on the cross for our sins.

2. Jesus **arose** from the tomb and is **alive** in heaven.

3. He tells us to trust in Him and not to be **afraid**.

4. The Bible tells us **about** many wonderful lessons.

✔ Divide these compound words.

treetop — tree-top   sailboats — sail-boats

milkweed — milk-weed   hillside — hill-side

playmate — play-mate   airway — air-way

beehive — bee-hive   beanbag — bean-bag

Using ✎ a and an

When one object is mentioned, the word **an** or **a** may be used when talking about that object.
1. The word **a** is used before a word that begins with a **consonant**: a car, a doll, or a tack.
2. The word **an** is used before a word that begins with a **vowel**: an ark, an egg, or an inch.

✔ Notice the beginning letter of each word and think of the rules above about **a** and **an**.

an apple	an oar	an object	a flute
a leaf	a church	a skunk	a shoe
an ant	an uncle	a block	a street
a boy	an elk	an ostrich	a dish
a pan	a twig	an eel	an egg

✔ Think as you print **a** or **an** in the blanks to complete the sentences.

1. Andrew can catch **a** leaf with his hands.

2. He feels **an** east wind is blowing the leaves.

3. His mother put his lunch in **a** brown bag.

4. He has **an** orange, **a** sandwich, and **a** cookie.

5. He saw **an** ant crawl up **a** tree and into **a** hole.

bicycle
pencil
giraffe
scissors
circle
faucet
fence
page

✔ What happens if e, i, or y comes after c or g? Print these soft c and soft g words.

giraffe   circle   scissors   faucet

bicycle   fence   page   pencil

Page 130

Purpose

1. To consider the letter **y** as a vowel when it comes at the end of words.

2. To learn that the **y** becomes a suffix when added to certain words as in **windy** and **chilly**.

Lesson

Carefully discuss with your student the rules about the vowel "y" as well as the lesson, and have him answer orally before he completes it independently.

Note: With respect to sentences 4 and 5 at the bottom of page130, their answers may be switced.

Page 131

Purpose

To review the lesson about the letter **y** being a vowel when it comes at the end of words.

Lesson

With your student, go over the rules about the vowel "y" as well as the lesson, and have him answer orally before he completes it independently.

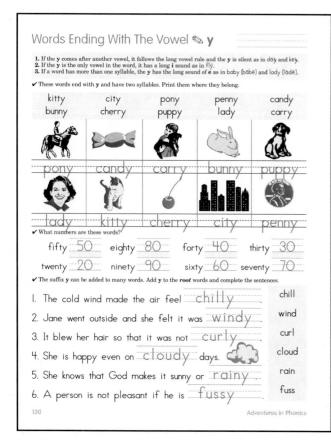

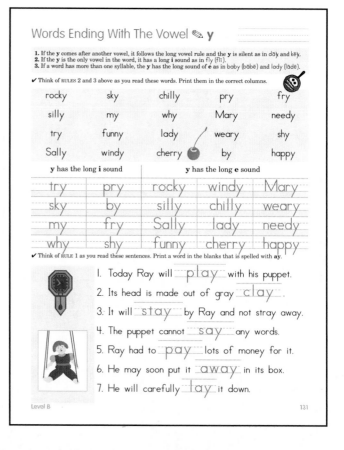

Page 132

Purpose
To teach the rules about making words ending with y to become *plural*.

Lesson
Thoroughly discuss the rules about making words, which end with the vowel **y**, become *plural* (more than one). Again, the student must know vowels from consonants. If this is the first lesson about plural words, go slowly to help him understand.

Have your student answer orally before he completes the page independently.

Page 133

Purpose
To give additional work in teaching the rules about making words ending with **y** to become *plural*.

Lesson
Thoroughly discuss the rules about making words, which end with the vowel **y**, become *plural* (more than one). Again, the student must know the difference between vowels and consonants. It is important that your student understands this lesson before he goes on to another page.

Have your student answer orally before he completes the page independently.

Plural Words Ending with ✎ y

An **s** is added to the end of many words when *more than one object* is mentioned (*plural*) as follows:
cat ⇒ cats   book ⇒ books   cake ⇒ cakes
If a word ends with **y**, two RULES need to be learned:
1. When the **y** follows a vowel, just add **s** as follows: **toy ⇒ toys, day ⇒ days,** and **key ⇒ keys.**

✔ Add **s** to make these words plural. Notice the vowel that comes before the ending **y**.

valley	valleys	day	days	turkey	turkeys
toy	toys	way	ways	key	keys
joy	joys	tray	trays	boy	boys

The second RULE for words ending with **y** is:
2. When the **y** follows a consonant, change the **y** to **i** and add **es**:
city ⇒ cities   baby ⇒ babies   pony ⇒ ponies

✔ Notice the consonant just before the ending **y**. Change the **y** to **i** and add **es** to these words.

lady	ladies	pony	ponies	puppy	puppies
copy	copies	lily	lilies	city	cities
story	stories	bunny	bunnies	duty	duties
penny	pennies	party	parties	candy	candies
fly	flies	worry	worries	kitty	kitties

✔ Notice if a vowel or consonant comes just before the ending **y**. Think of the two rules above.

1. Brad saw two brown ponies in the yard.
2. He saw them run and play for three days.
3. He gathered a basket of berries to eat.
4. Brad picked some lilies for his mother.
5. He knows that God made the green valleys.

lily
day
berry
valley
pony

132   Adventures in Phonics

Plural Words Ending With ✎ y

An **s** is added to the end of many words when *more than one object* is mentioned (*plural*) as follows:
cat ⇒ cats   book ⇒ books   cake ⇒ cakes
If a word ends with **y**, two RULES need to be learned:
1. When the **y** follows a vowel, just add **s** as follows: **toy ⇒ toys, day ⇒ days,** and **key ⇒ keys.**
2. When the **y** follows a consonant, change the **y** to **i** and add **es**:
city ⇒ cities   baby ⇒ babies   pony ⇒ ponies

✔ What letter comes before **y**? Think about these RULES as you make the words to become plural.

penny	pennies	lily	lilies	cherry	cherries
valley	valleys	fly	flies	tray	trays
baby	babies	supply	supplies	berry	berries
toy	toys	donkey	donkeys	key	keys
turkey	turkeys	pony	ponies	lady	ladies
story	stories	boy	boys	daisy	daisies

✔ Now print these words to be singular or mean *only one*.

turkeys	turkey	stories	story	flies	fly
babies	baby	joys	joy	keys	key
bunnies	bunny	ladies	lady	cities	city

✔ Make the words plural to complete the sentences.

1. A nickel is the same as five pennies.
2. The farmer had six cows and ten turkeys.
3. Jerry had three pears and six cherries.
4. Our class has ten girls and ten boys.

turkey
boy
cherry
penny

Level B   133

Page 134

Purpose

To teach the rule about making words that end with **s**, **x**, **z**, **ch**, and **sh** *plural*.

Lesson

Print the following chart on the board or have your student look at this page. Have him say the underlined letters several times. Teach him this rule:

If a word ends with **s**, **x**, **z**, **ch**, or **sh**, the letters **-es** are added to make that word *plural*.

s	*x*	*z*	*sh*	*ch*
cross	box	buzz	bush	arch
crosses	boxes	buzzes	bushes	arches
glass	ax	fizz	crash	latch
glasses	axes	fizzes	crashes	latches
miss	tax	waltz	dish	lunch
misses	taxes	waltzes	dishes	lunches

Carefully go over the lesson and have your student answer orally before he completes the work independently.

Page 135

Purpose

To teach about adding suffixes **ly** and **er** to root words.

Lesson

Print the suffixes **-ly** and **-er** on the board. As you pronounce them, say that each suffix has a vowel sound: the **-ly** has the consonant **l** and a long **e** sound, and the **-er** has the *schwa* plus **r** sound as it is heard in words such as **work<u>er</u>**, **runn<u>er</u>**, and **help<u>er</u>**.

Print these words on the board. After your student has read them, add the suffix **-ly** to them and have him read the words again.

quick   poor   glad   soft

Print these words on the board. After they have been read, add the suffix **-er** to them and have the student read the words again.

quick   soft   fast   work

Refer to the ending letters **-ly** and **-er** as *suffixes*.

Carefully go over the lesson and have your student answer orally before he completes the work independently.

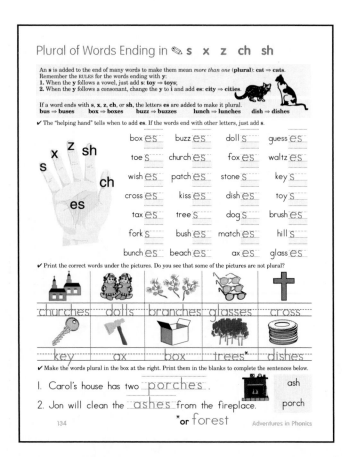

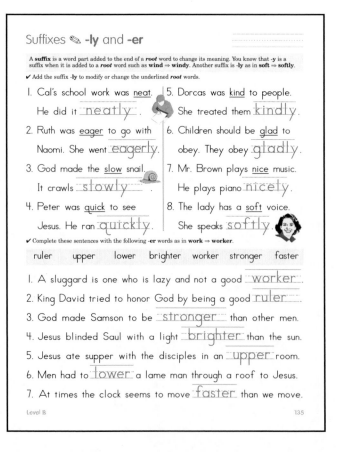

Page 136

Purpose

1. To teach more about **suffixes**.

2. To introduce the definition of **syllable**.

Lesson

Review the meaning of a **suffix**: letters added to the end of a root word to change its meaning.

A **syllable** is a word or part of a word with a vowel sound which is pronounced with a single sound.

Print these words on the board and say them to your student. Clap for each *syllable*:

sis•ter   sum•mer   sil•ver

Each part or *syllable* of these words has a vowel sound. Pronounce and clap the names of other objects that are in your room:

ta•ble   pup•py   moth•er
ba•by   pen•cil   fa•ther
win•dow   cov•er   doc•tor

Carefully go over the lesson and have your student answer orally before he completes the work independently.

Page 137

Purpose

To teach about the suffix **-ful**.

Lesson

Introduce the suffix **-ful** and mention that it has a vowel sound. This means that it is also a *syllable* when it is at the end of a word.

This is an easy lesson, but carefully go over it and have the student answer orally before he does the work by himself.

Suffixes and Syllables ✎ er, or, and ar

Suffixes are letters added to the end of a *root* word to change its meaning as in **work ⇒ worker**.
A **syllable** is a word or part of a word with a vowel sound which is pronounced with a single sound.
   cab ⇒ cabin   rob ⇒ robin   win ⇒ winter   late ⇒ later

✔ Complete these sentences with the following -er words. The **er** is part of the last syllable in each word.

answer	brother	bitter	silver	winter

1. Thad's little **brother** found a **silver** coin.

2. We should speak kindly when we give an **answer**.

3. The weather had **bitter** winds during this **winter**.

✔ These words end with **or** and **ar** which make the *ǝr* or *schwa* plus **r** sound.
Complete the following sentences with the **or** and **ar** words in the box. Print them in the blanks below.

doctor	tailor	caterpillar	cellar
beggar	dollar	binoculars	anchor

1. When our neighbor got sick we called a **doctor**.

2. The sailor uses a pair of **binoculars** to see.

3. Jesus healed the **beggar** who had been born blind.

4. Bill had a **tailor** fix the collar on his suit.

5. Jill found a **caterpillar** with pretty colors.

✔ Drop the **s** or **es** and add **or** to modify these words. **The One who creates is The Creator.**

1. One who instructs is an **instructor**

2. One who collects is a **collector**

3. One who directs is a **director**

4. One who operates is an **operator**

136   Adventures in Phonics

Suffix ✎ -ful

REMEMBER: **Suffixes** are letters added to the end of a word to change its meaning.
The suffix **-ful** means *full of*. The **u** makes a vowel sound, so **-ful** is a syllable.

✔ Carefully add the suffix **ful** and read your new words.

peace	**peaceful**	fear	**fearful**	shame	**shameful**
use	**useful**	care	**careful**	need	**needful**
hope	**hopeful**	skill	**skillful**	rest	**restful**
watch	**watchful**	truth	**truthful**	pain	**painful**

✔ Print these words where they belong to complete the sentences.

cheerful	helpful	faithful	powerful	playful	careful

1. The little brown puppy was **playful**.

2. We should be **cheerful** as we help others.

3. Tara tries to be **helpful** to her mother.

4. We should be **careful** as we print.

5. God is always **faithful** to His people.

6. He is all **powerful**; with Him nothing is impossible.

A good neighbor is
helpful
thoughtful
thankful
useful
careful
truthful
faithful
cheerful

✔ Match the phrases in the left-hand columns with the correct **-ful** words in the right-hand columns.

He who tells the truth is	restful.	One who thanks is	careful.
One who is resting is	truthful.	One who takes care is	cheerful.
One who helps is	fearful.	One who has cheer is	thankful.
Someone who fears is	skillful.	A sore that has pain is	useful.
One who has skill is	helpful.	A thing that is of use is	painful.

Level B   137

Page 138

Purpose

To teach about the suffixes **-less** and **-ness**.

Lesson

Introduce the suffixes **-less** and **-ness** and mention that they each have a vowel sound—the short vowel sound of **e**. This means that they are *syllables* when they are at the end of words.

Carefully go over the lesson and listen to the student answer orally before he does the work by himself.

Page 139

Purpose

To teach the meaning the suffixes **-er** and **-est** have when added to words.

Lesson

Introduce the suffixes **-er** and **-est** and mention that they also have the short vowel sound of **e** and are *syllables*. Explain the meanings they have by printing these words on the board.

root	*er*	*est*
soft	softer	softest
hard	harder	hardest

These *suffixes* help us to tell about differences as we speak.

Bill is tall,
Will is tall<u>er</u>,
but Phil is tall<u>est</u>.

Carefully go over the lesson and listen as your student answers orally before he does the work by himself.

Suffixes ✎ -less and -ness

REMEMBER: **Suffixes** are letters added to the end of a word to change its meaning. The suffix **-less** means *without* or *not*. The **e** makes a vowel sound, so **-less** is a syllable.

✔ Be careful as you add the suffix **-less** and read your new words.

care	careless	worth	worthless	bone	boneless
use	useless	blame	blameless	tire	tireless
spot	spotless	thought	thoughtless	end	endless

✔ Match these words with opposite meanings.

fearless — careful | painless — useful | faithful — harmful
careless — hopeless | useless — painful | thankful — faithless
hopeful — fearful | helpful — helpless | harmless — thankless

✔ Add **-less** and read the new words.

without faith	faithless	without harm	harmless
without care	careless	without power	powerless
without shame	shameless	without hope	hopeless

The suffix **-ness** tells about a condition or state of being: **sad** ⇒ **sadness**.

✔ Carefully add the suffix **-ness** as you read your new words. Print the correct words in the blanks below.

quick	quickness	sick	sickness	slow	slowness
kind	kindness	sweet	sweetness	sad	sadness
neat	neatness	ill	illness	soft	softness

1. The neighbors showed kindness during Carl's illness* .

2. Miss Ellen's life is full of thoughtfulness and kindness** .

3. The opposite of quickness is slowness .

138   *or sickness **or sweetness

Suffixes ✎ -er and -est

The suffix **-er** is added to words to compare *two* things: **fast** ⇒ **faster**.
The suffix **-est** is added to words to compare *more than two* things: **tall** ⇒ **taller** ⇒ **tallest**.

✔ Neatly add the suffixes **-er** and **-est** to form new words.

	-er	-est		-er	-est
kind	kinder	kindest	wild	wilder	wildest
long	longer	longest	high	higher	highest
short	shorter	shortest	tall	taller	tallest
clear	clearer	clearest	old	older	oldest
thick	thicker	thickest	cold	colder	coldest
slow	slower	slowest	fast	faster	fastest
small	smaller	smallest	quick	quicker	quickest

✔ Add the suffixes **-er** or **-est** to complete these sentences.

1. An elephant is one of the strongest animals. (strong)

2. Judy is shorter than her older brother and sister. (short)

3. A giraffe is one of the tallest animals God created. (tall)

4. Nathan runs faster than any of the boys on the team. (fast)

5. Pat's kite flew the highest of all the children. (high)

6. Summer is the warmest time of the year. (warm)

7. God made the hummingbird smaller than the wren. (small)

8. The turtle is one of the slowest animals in the world. (slow)

Level B   139

Page 140

Purpose

To teach the three sounds that suffix **-ed** has.

Lesson

Print these columns of words on the board or have your student read from this page. Tell him that **-ed** can say three different sounds. As he reads down the lists, have him listen to the sounds made by the **-ed**.

d	t	ed
called	mixed	rested
climbed	jumped	hunted
sailed	hiked	treated
peeled	thanked	folded

Your student may need to go over this again if it was difficult for him. It may help if he claps as he pronounces the words. In the third column the "ed" has the *schwa* sound which means it is a *syllable*; therefore, the words would need two claps.

Carefully go over the lesson and listen as your student answers orally before he does the work by himself.

Page 141

Purpose

To teach the rule about adding a **suffix** that begins with a vowel to a word with a short vowel.

Lesson

As you teach the rule written on the top of the page, print these words on the board or have your student look at this page.

If a one-syllable word with a short vowel ends with **one** consonant, **double** that consonant before adding a suffix that begins with a vowel.

root	ed	ing
hop	hopped	hopping
step	stepped	stepping
drip	dripped	dripping
rub	rubbed	rubbing

Ask your student to tell you how many consonants are at the end of the words in the first column above. Ask him if the last letter of these short vowel words below should be doubled.

jump   stamp   land   spill

No! They end with two consonants.

Sounds of Suffix ✎ -ed

The suffix **-ed** can make three different sounds:
d as in **cheered** and **called**; **t** as in **fixed** and **worked**; and **ed** as in **printed** and **handed**.
Conrad call**ed** his father.   The man work**ed** hard.   Tom print**ed** neatly.

✔ As you read these words, underline the **-ed** sound. Print the sound **-ed** makes in the blanks: **d**, **t**, or **ed**.

turned	d	squirted	ed	jumped	t		
fixed	t	finished	t	climbed	d		
handed	ed	asked	t	hunted	ed		
served	d	scolded	ed	pushed	t		
rushed	t	weeded	ed	groaned	d		
called	d	learned	d	planted	ed		

Every syllable has a vowel sound. When the **-ed** sounds like **ed**, it makes another syllable as in **handed**.

✔ Listen to the suffix **-ed** and print how many syllables each word has.

pulled	1	searched	1	called	1
handed	2	carted	2	folded	2
thanked	1	finished	2	greeted	2
cheered	1	walked	1	burned	1

✔ Circle the numeral for the sentences that may be true.

1. Jeff and his sister do not like to read.
2. He is reading a book on plants.
3. He enjoys reading in his home.
4. A horse is reading a big book about hay.
5. Renee is reading about pretty flowers.

140   Adventures in Phonics

✎ Adding Suffixes

If a one-syllable word with a short vowel ends with **one** consonant, **double** the consonant before adding a suffix that begins with a vowel: hop ⇒ hopped ⇒ hopper ⇒ hopping ⇒ hoppy.

✔ Remember to double the ending consonant as you add these suffixes to the short vowel words.

	-ed	-ing		-er	-est
nap	napped	napping	hot	hotter	hottest
shop	shopped	shopping	mad	madder	maddest
rub	rubbed	rubbing	big	bigger	biggest
drip	dripped	dripping	thin	thinner	thinnest
scrub	scrubbed	scrubbing	fat	fatter	fattest
step	stepped	stepping	dim	dimmer	dimmest
tap	tapped	tapping	wet	wetter	wettest

✔ Read the rule again before you add suffixes to these short vowel words. REMEMBER: **y** may be a vowel.

swim + ing = swimming	stick + y = sticky
scrub + er = scrubber	fog + y = foggy
jump + ing = jumping	stiff + est = stiffest
shag + y = shaggy	pick + ing = picking
flat + er = flatter	stamp + ed = stamped
trim + ing = trimming	win + er = winner
fill + ed = filled	drip + ing = dripping

✔ Underline the suffixes in the following sentence.

A fluffy squirrel jump**ed** and hopp**ed** while gather**ing** nuts.

Level B   141

Page 142

Purpose
To teach about **suffixes** and words that end with **e**.

Lesson
Review the rule you studied in the last lesson:

If a one-syllable word with a short vowel ends with **one** consonant, double that consonant before adding a suffix that begins with a vowel.

<u>rub</u>bed <u>tap</u>ped <u>hop</u>ped <u>tip</u>ped

This lesson has another important rule:

When a word ends with a silent **e**, drop the **e** before adding a suffix that begins with a vowel.

root	*ed*	*ing*
joke	joked	joking
close	closed	closing
hope	hoped	hoping
smile	smiled	smiling

When your student understands this rule, carefully go over the lesson and listen as he answers orally before he does the work by himself.

Page 143

Purpose
To review the **suffix rules** of the past two lessons.

Lesson
Review these rules:

If a one-syllable word with a short vowel ends with **one** consonant, *double* that consonant before adding a suffix.

fat   big   hit   sun
<u>fat</u>ter <u>big</u>gest <u>hit</u>ting <u>sun</u>ny

These words are divided into *syllables* between the double consonants if the suffix has a vowel sound.

fat-ter big-gest hit-ting sun-ny

When a word ends with a silent **e**, drop the **e** before adding a suffix that begins with a vowel.

hide   wave   late   drive
hiding   waved   latest   driver

When your student understands these rules, carefully go over the lesson and listen as he answers orally before he does the work by himself.

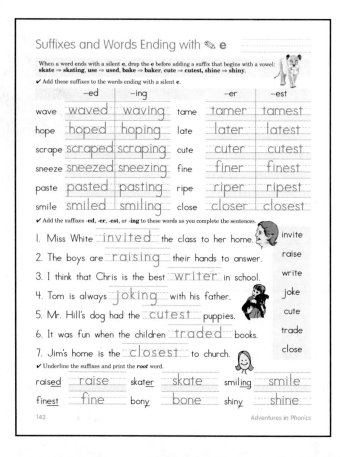

Suffixes and Words Ending with ✎ e

When a word ends with a silent e, drop the e before adding a suffix that begins with a vowel:
skate ⇒ skating, use ⇒ used, bake ⇒ baker, cute ⇒ cutest, shine ⇒ shiny.

✔ Add these suffixes to the words ending with a silent e.

	-ed	-ing		-er	-est
wave	waved	waving	tame	tamer	tamest
hope	hoped	hoping	late	later	latest
scrape	scraped	scraping	cute	cuter	cutest
sneeze	sneezed	sneezing	fine	finer	finest
paste	pasted	pasting	ripe	riper	ripest
smile	smiled	smiling	close	closer	closest

✔ Add the suffixes **-ed, -er, -est,** or **-ing** to these words as you complete the sentences.

1. Miss White invited the class to her home.   invite

2. The boys are raising their hands to answer.   raise

3. I think that Chris is the best writer in school.   write

4. Tom is always joking with his father.   joke

5. Mr. Hill's dog had the cutest puppies.   cute

6. It was fun when the children traded books.   trade

7. Jim's home is the closest to church.   close

✔ Underline the suffixes and print the *root* word.

raised raise   skater skate   smiling smile
finest fine   bony bone   shiny shine

142   Adventures in Phonics

✎ Review of Suffixes

When adding a suffix beginning with a <u>vowel</u> (**-ed, -er, -ing, -est,** or **-y**) remember two RULES:
1. If a one-syllable word with a <u>short vowel</u> ends with *one* consonant, *double* that consonant before adding a suffix: **nap ⇒ napped, tap ⇒ tapping, fat ⇒ fattest, wet ⇒ wetter,** and **mud ⇒ muddy.**
2. If a word ends with a silent **e** drop the e before adding a suffix: **wave ⇒ waving** and **late ⇒ later.**

✔ Add the suffixes **-er** and **-est** to these short vowel words as you complete the sentences.

1. My cat is <u>fat</u>, Jan's is fatter, but Ted's is fattest.

2. Levi is <u>tall</u>, Ben is taller, but Sam is tallest.

3. Ed's cup is <u>full</u>, Al's is fuller, but mine is fullest.

4. My dog is <u>big</u>, Jill's is bigger, but Kay's is biggest.

5. Jay is <u>kind</u>, Glen is kinder, but Mike is kindest.

✔ Add the suffixes **-er** and **-est** to these words which end with e as you complete the sentences.

1. Jon came <u>late</u>, Will came later, but Todd came latest.

2. The pear is <u>ripe</u>, the apple is riper, but the plum is ripest.

3. Our bird is <u>tame</u>, our cat is tamer, but our dog is tamest.

4. Tim lives <u>close</u>, Gail lives closer, Don lives closest.

5. Dirt is <u>fine</u>, sand is finer, but flour is finest.

✔ Add the suffix **-y**, which is a vowel, to these words. REMEMBER the rules above.

flop	floppy	drip	drippy
bug	buggy	rose	rosy
sun	sunny	stone	stony
grease	greasy	taste	tasty

Level B   143

Page 144

Purpose

To review the **suffix rules** of the past lessons.

Lesson

Review these rules:

If a one-syllable word with a short vowel ends with *one* consonant, *double* that consonant before adding a suffix.

clip	hug	tip	mud
clip**p**er	hug**g**ed	tip**p**ing	mud**d**y

These words are divided into *syllables* between the double consonants if the suffix has a vowel sound.

clip-per hug-ged tip-ping mud-dy

When a word ends with a silent **e**, drop the **e** before adding a suffix that begins with a vowel.

bake	rose	wise	smile
baker	rosy	wiser	smiled

When your student understands these rules, carefully go over the lesson and listen as he answers orally before he does the work by himself.

Page 145

Purpose

To review the **suffix rules** of the past lessons.

Lesson

Thoroughly review the four rules at the top of the student's page. Suggest that he look at the root words to help him decide how to add the suffixes.

When you think that your student understands these rules, carefully go over the lesson and listen as he answers orally before he does the work by himself.

As is suggested for all of the lessons, correct his work the same day it is completed, talk about any errors, and have them corrected right away.

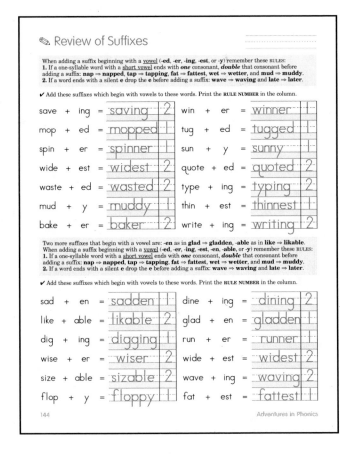

✎ Review of Suffixes

When adding a suffix beginning with a <u>vowel</u> (-**ed**, -**er**, -**ing**, -**est**, or -**y**) remember these RULES:
1. If a one-syllable word with a <u>short vowel</u> ends with *one* consonant, *double* that consonant before adding a suffix: **nap ⇒ napped, tap ⇒ tapping, fat ⇒ fattest, wet ⇒ wetter**, and **mud ⇒ muddy.**
2. If a word ends with a silent **e** drop the **e** before adding a suffix: **wave ⇒ waving** and **late ⇒ later.**

✔ Add these suffixes which begin with vowels to these words. Print the RULE NUMBER in the column.

save + ing = saving	2	win + er = winner	1
mop + ed = mopped	1	tug + ed = tugged	1
spin + er = spinner	1	sun + y = sunny	1
wide + est = widest	2	quote + ed = quoted	2
waste + ed = wasted	2	type + ing = typing	2
mud + y = muddy	1	thin + est = thinnest	1
bake + er = baker	2	write + ing = writing	2

Two more suffixes that begin with a vowel are: -**en** as in **glad ⇒ gladden**, -**able** as in **like ⇒ likable**. When adding a suffix beginning with a <u>vowel</u> (-**ed**, -**er**, -**ing**, -**est**, -**able**, or -**y**) remember these RULES:
1. If a one-syllable word with a <u>short vowel</u> ends with *one* consonant, *double* that consonant before adding a suffix: **nap ⇒ napped, tap ⇒ tapping, fat ⇒ fattest, wet ⇒ wetter**, and **mud ⇒ muddy.**
2. If a word ends with a silent **e** drop the **e** before adding a suffix: **wave ⇒ waving** and **late ⇒ later.**

✔ Add these suffixes which begin with vowels to these words. Print the RULE NUMBER in the column.

sad + en = sadden	1	dine + ing = dining	2
like + able = likable	2	glad + en = gladden	1
dig + ing = digging	1	run + er = runner	1
wise + er = wiser	2	wide + est = widest	2
size + able = sizable	2	wave + ing = waving	2
flop + y = floppy	1	fat + est = fattest	1

144   Adventures in Phonics

✎ Review of Suffixes

When adding a suffix beginning with a <u>vowel</u> (-**ed**, -**er**, -**ing**, -**est**, -**en**, -**able**, or -**y**), remember these RULES:

1. If a one-syllable word with a <u>short vowel</u> ends with *one* consonant, *double* that consonant before adding a suffix: **nap ⇒ napped**	**2.** If a word ends with a silent **e**, drop the **e** before adding a suffix beginning with a vowel: **wave ⇒ waving**	**3.** If a <u>short vowel</u> word ends with **two** consonants just add the suffix beginning with a vowel: **jump ⇒ jumping**	**4.** If a word has a <u>long vowel</u> sound just add the suffix beginning with a vowel: **rain ⇒ rained**

✔ Add these suffixes which begin with vowels to these words. Print the RULE NUMBER in the column.

brave + est = bravest	2	bump + ing = bumping	3
shop + ed = shopped	1	run + er = runner	1
camp + er = camper	3	like + able = likable	2
snow + ed = snowed	4	fill + ing = filling	3
plan + ed = planned	1	paint + ing = painting	4
rose + y = rosy	2	sad + en = sadden	1
pose + ing = posing	2	crisp + y = crispy	3

To add a suffix beginning with a <u>consonant</u> (-**less**, -**ness**, -**ly**, or -**ful**), usually no change is needed.

✔ Add the suffixes -**less**, -**ness**, -**ly**, or -**ful** to these words. Remember the rule above.

lone + ly = lonely	cup + ful = cupful
kind + ness = kindness	glad + ness = gladness
cheer + ful = cheerful	slow + ly = slowly
care + less = careless	doubt + less = doubtless
pain + ful = painful	red + ness = redness
bone + less = boneless	joy + ful = joyful

Level B   145

Page 146

Purpose

To review the three rules about adding *suffixes* to words ending with **y**.

Lesson

Review the rules one at a time on the top of the worksheet. Look at each section that matches that rule and use the words for examples. The words in each section match the rule, so the student will not have to decide which rule to apply. However, applying the rule to each word orally should strengthen his understanding.

When your student has a strong understanding of the rules, have him print the answers.

Page 147

Purpose

To review the three rules about adding **suffixes** to words ending with **y**.

Lesson

Repeat your lesson of reviewing the rules one at a time on the top of the worksheet. Looking back at each section on the previous page may be helpful for examples. The words in the top section are varied, so the student will have to think about the rule to apply to the *root* word.

When your student has a good understanding of the rules and has given the answers orally, have him complete the lesson in pencil.

Words Ending With ✎ y

Why does the "y" need special attention?

1. If a word ends with a **y** next to a <u>consonant</u>, we usually change the **y** to **i** and add the suffix: **try ⇒ tried, carry ⇒ carrier, story ⇒ stories, beauty ⇒ beautiful**, and **penny ⇒ penniless**.
2. DO NOT change the **y** when a <u>vowel</u> comes before it: **play ⇒ played, gray ⇒ grayest**.
3. DO NOT change the **y** when adding the suffix **ing**: **carry ⇒ carrying, play ⇒ playing**.

✔ Add these suffixes to the words which end with a **y**.

heavy + ness = heaviness	copy + er = copier
happy + est = happiest	cry + es = cries
merry + ly = merrily	plenty + ful = plentiful
marry + ed = married	cozy + er = cozier
dry + est = driest	sorry + est = sorriest
ready + ness = readiness	hurry + ed = hurried

✔ Add these suffixes to the words. Remember! DO NOT change the **y** if a vowel comes before it.

play + ful = playful	joy + ful = joyful
pray + er = prayer	obey + ed = obeyed
gray + est = grayest	pay + able = payable
plenty + ful = plentiful	cry + es = cries

✔ Add the suffix **-ing** to these words. Remember! DO NOT change the **y** when adding the suffix **-ing**.

stay staying	obey obeying	cry crying
pray praying	carry carrying	say saying
try trying	worry worrying	hurry hurrying
marry marrying	play playing	copy copying

146   Adventures in Phonics

Words Ending With ✎ y

How do you add a suffix to a word ending with a "y"?

1. If a word ends with a **y** next to a <u>consonant</u>, we usually change the **y** to **i** and add the suffix: **try ⇒ tried, carry ⇒ carrier, story ⇒ stories, beauty ⇒ beautiful**, and **penny ⇒ penniless**.
2. DO NOT change the **y** when a <u>vowel</u> comes before it: **play ⇒ played, gray ⇒ grayest**.
3. DO NOT change the **y** when adding the suffix **ing**: **carry ⇒ carrying, play ⇒ playing**.

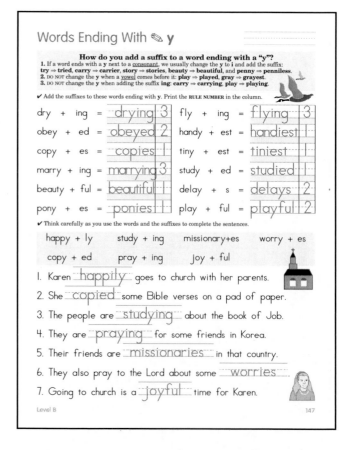

✔ Add the suffixes to these words ending with **y**. Print the RULE NUMBER in the column.

dry + ing =	drying	3	fly + ing =	flying	3
obey + ed =	obeyed	2	handy + est =	handiest	1
copy + es =	copies	1	tiny + est =	tiniest	1
marry + ing =	marrying	3	study + ed =	studied	1
beauty + ful =	beautiful	1	delay + s =	delays	2
pony + es =	ponies	1	play + ful =	playful	2

✔ Think carefully as you use the words and the suffixes to complete the sentences.

happy + ly	study + ing	missionary+es	worry + es
copy + ed	pray + ing	joy + ful	

1. Karen happily goes to church with her parents.
2. She copied some Bible verses on a pad of paper.
3. The people are studying about the book of Job.
4. They are praying for some friends in Korea.
5. Their friends are missionaries in that country.
6. They also pray to the Lord about some worries.
7. Going to church is a joyful time for Karen.

Level B   147

Page 148

Purpose

To review the **suffix rules** of the past lessons.

Lesson

Review the rules on this lesson one at a time, using the words in the sections as examples. Help the student to understand that a suffix can be divided from the root word if that suffix has a vowel sound. Notice these words. Some of the words should not be divided. As the words are pronounced, a reader should be able to sense the division.

s	ed	er	ing
jumps	jumped	jump-er	jump-ing
tests	test-ed	test-er	test-ing
hauls	hauled	haul-er	haul-ing

When the lesson has been answered orally, have the student complete it independently.

Page 149

Purpose

1. To review the **suffix rules** of the past lessons.

2. To divide compound words.

Lesson

Review this rule:

A *suffix* is a syllable in itself if it has a vowel sound.

eat-ing   sleep-y   soft-est   knock-er

Review this rule:

A *suffix* should not be divided from the root word if the suffix does not have a vowel sound.

desks   shopped   thinks   smiled

When the lesson has been answered orally, have the student complete it independently.

✎ Review of Words with Suffixes

A **suffix** is a syllable in itself if it has a vowel sound as in **fly-ing**, **bone-less**, **land-ed**, and **lunch-es**.

✔ Divide these words into syllables. Do you hear the vowel sound that is in each of these suffixes?

praying	pray-ing	kindness	kind-ness
newest	new-est	speaker	speak-er
helpful	help-ful	painting	paint-ing
sadly	sad-ly	thoughtful	thought-ful
slower	slow-er	softest	soft-est
harmless	harm-less	darkness	dark-ness
tested	test-ed	wisely	wise-ly

A **suffix** is a syllable in itself if it has a vowel sound as in **fly-ing**, **bone-less**, **land-ed**, and **lunch-es**. Never divide a combination of letters that are pronounced as one syllable as in **jumped** or **looks**.

✔ Divide these words into syllables. Watch for words with suffixes that should not be divided.

treated	treat-ed	helper	help-er
feared	feared	smallest	small-est
reading	read-ing	trusted	trust-ed
careful	care-ful	greedy	greed-y
works	works	called	called

✔ Underline the words in these verses that have suffixes.

• <u>Blessed</u> is the man who always <u>fears</u> the Lord. (Proverbs 28:14a)

• Make a <u>joyful</u> noise unto God. (Psalm 66:1a)

• A <u>faithful</u> man will be <u>richly</u> <u>blessed</u>. Proverbs 28:20a)

148   Adventures in Phonics

✎ Review of Words with Suffixes

A **suffix** is a syllable in itself if it has a vowel sound as in **fly-ing**, **bone-less**, **land-ed**, and **lunch-es**.

✔ Each of the sentences have *two* words with **suffixes**. Underline the words and divide them as you print them. Watch for words with suffixes that should not be divided.

		1 Syllable Words	2 Syllable Words
1. Chuck <u>wants</u> to be <u>helpful</u> to dad.		wants	help-ful
2. He <u>thinks</u> about the Bible <u>teaching</u>.		thinks	teach-ing
3. He is <u>blessed</u> when he is <u>praying</u>.		blessed	pray-ing
4. They are <u>watching</u> his good <u>works</u>.		works	watch-ing
5. You will be <u>thinking</u> about her <u>deeds</u>.		deeds	think-ing
6. He <u>knows</u> a <u>lying</u> word will hurt them.		knows	ly-ing

REMEMBER! If a word ends with **s**, **x**, **z**, **ch**, or **sh**, add **es** to make it plural:
bus ⇒ **buses**, **box** ⇒ **boxes**, **buzz** ⇒ **buzzes**, **lunch** ⇒ **lunches**, and **dish** ⇒ **dishes**.

✔ The **e** makes a vowel sound which makes **es** to be a syllable. Divide these words.

catches	catch-es	marches	march-es
mixes	mix-es	taxes	tax-es
dishes	dish-es	dresses	dress-es
reaches	reach-es	buzzes	buzz-es

✔ Divide these compound words.

footprints	foot-prints	stairway	stair-way
highway	high-way	popcorn	pop-corn
tonight	to-night	necktie	neck-tie
something	some-thing	beanbag	bean-bag

Level B   149

Page 150

Purpose

1. To teach about the prefixes **un-** and **dis-**.

2. To work with words with opposite meanings.

Lesson

Explain the **prefix rule** at the top of the lesson, using the words in that section for examples.

When your student has a good understanding of the page and has given the answers orally, have him complete the lesson in pencil.

Page 151

Purpose

To teach about the prefixes **re-**, **de-**, and **pre-**.

Lesson

Discuss the definition of a **prefix** as it is explained in the rule at the top of the lesson, using the words in that section for examples.

When your student has given the answers orally and has a good understanding of the page, have him complete the lesson in pencil.

Prefixes ✎ un- and dis-

A **prefix** is a syllable placed before a **root** word to change its meaning as in **unhappy** and **disagree**. The prefixes **un-** and **dis-** are usually opposite the meaning of the **root** word.

✔ Underline the **root** word and draw a circle around the prefix. Print the root word on the line.

disappear	appear	unfair	fair
unscrew	screw	displease	please
dislocate	locate	unwilling	willing
unkind	kind	unsafe	safe
unhappy	happy	disobey	obey
dishonest	honest	unknown	known
untrue	true	dislike	like

✔ Match the words which have the opposite meaning.

agree — unjust   order — unpin   screw — untrue
certain — unhappy   known — dishonest   please — dislocate
just — unfold   fair — disobey   willing — unsafe
happy — dislike   pin — unknown   true — unscrew
fold — disagree   honest — disorder   locate — displease
like — uncertain   obey — unfair   safe — unwilling

✔ Print the word with a **prefix** which has the meaning of the underlined words.

1. Jim was <u>not willing</u> to be dishonest.   unwilling

2. It is wrong when a person is <u>not kind</u> to his pet.   unkind

3. The Lord is <u>not happy</u> if we disobey our parents.   unhappy

4. God is just; He is angry if people are <u>not fair</u>.   unfair

---

Prefixes ✎ re-, de-, and pre-

A **prefix** is a syllable placed before a **root** word to change its meaning as in **retype**, **defrost**, and **prefix**. The prefix **re-** usually means **do again**. The prefix **de-** usually means **from**. The prefix **pre-** usually means **before** or **ahead**.

✔ Divide these words which have prefixes.

defrost	de-frost	rebuild	re-build
reread	re-read	preview	pre-view
detour	de-tour	remake	re-make
preschool	pre-school	detest	de-test
depart	de-part	retell	re-tell
refile	re-file	replant	re-plant
rewash	re-wash	prewar	pre-war

These words also begin with the syllables **re-**, **de-**, and **pre-** as in **remind**, **decide**, and **prevent**.

✔ Read this list and use the underlined words to complete the sentences.

<u>prepares</u>	recess	<u>pretend</u>	present	<u>delicious</u>
rejoice	<u>receive</u>	<u>decides</u>	<u>remind</u>	depend

1. Conrad can smell the delicious food in the kitchen.

2. He is happy that his mother prepares such tasty meals.

3. His father never has to remind him to wash his hands.

4. He does not need to pretend that he is hungry.

5. His family always thanks God for the food they receive.

6. After dinner he decides to do homework before playing.

Page 152

Purpose
To teach about the prefixes **ex-**, **fore-**, and **for-**.

Lesson
Discuss the definitions of prefixes **ex-**, **fore-**, and **for-** as explained in the rules at the top of the lesson.

When your student has given the answers orally and has a good understanding of the page, have him complete the lesson in pencil.

Page 153

Purpose
To teach about the prefix **be-**.

Lesson
Introduce the prefix **be-**, using the words in the exercise box for examples.

When your student has given the answers orally and has a good understanding of the page, have him complete the lesson in pencil.

Prefixes ✎ ex-, fore-, and for-

A **prefix** is a syllable placed before a **root** word to change its meaning as in **exit** and **forenoon**.
The prefix **ex-** usually means **from** or **out of** as in **ex-tent** and **ex-it**.
The prefix **fore-** usually means **before** in time or place as in **fore-noon**.
The prefix **for-** usually means **away, apart,** or **off** as in **for-bid**.

✔ Read and divide these words into syllables.

forefinger	fore-fin-ger	forefather	fore-fa-ther
expand	ex-pand	excuse	ex-cuse
foretell	fore-tell	forbid	for-bid
forgive	for-give	forehead	fore-head
exclaim	ex-claim	explain	ex-plain
forward	for-ward	express	ex-press
exchange	ex-change	forget	for-get

✔ Circle the **prefixes** as you read these words. Use the underlined words to complete the sentences below.

(expel) (foreknow) (extend) (forewarn) (forearm)
(forever) (foreground) (forecast) (extract) (explode)

1. We will be happy as we live in heaven with God forever.
2. Only our great Lord can foreknow the future.
3. When Kevin fell he got a cut on his left forearm.
4. Our family heard the weather forecast on the radio.
5. The vet had to extract a broken tooth from a monkey.
6. The policeman had to expel the rude boy from the store.

152   Adventures in Phonics

Prefix ✎ be-   Suffix and Prefix Review

A **prefix** is a syllable placed before a **root** word to change its meaning.
A **suffix** is a letter or group of letters added to the end of a **root** word to change its meaning.

✔ Read aloud the following words which begin with the syllable or prefix **be-**.
Divide these words into syllables and use them in the sentences below.

be-low be-lieve be-longs be-have be-ware
be-gins be-hind be-neath be-side be-fore

1. Everyone should believe in God and the Bible.
2. I kneel beside my desk to pray as school begins.
3. The duck flew below or beneath the clouds.
4. We honor our parents when we behave as we should.
5. A rabbit ran behind the shed before Wag could get it.
6. We should beware of being a lazy person.
7. We should not take anything that belongs to others.

✔ These words have **prefixes** and **suffixes**. Read and divide these words into syllables.

preschooler	pre-school-er	replanted	re-plant-ed
untruthful	un-truth-ful	departed	de-part-ed
remaining	re-main-ing	unfairly	un-fair-ly
retested	re-test-ed	explaining	ex-plain-ing
unpacking	un-pack-ing	unscrewing	un-screw-ing
unwisely	un-wise-ly	defrosted	de-frost-ed
previewing	pre-view-ing	rereading	re-read-ing

Level B   153

Page 154

Purpose
To teach the rules regarding one-syllable words and compound words.

Lesson
Review the definition of a *syllable*.

A syllable is a word or part of a word with one vowel sound and is pronounced with a single sound of the voice.

hand   door   tree   straight

Because these words have only one vowel sound, **Rule One** states:

A one-syllable word must never be divided.

Since compound words are made up of two or more words, **Rule Two** says:

Divide a compound word between the words that make the compound word.

grape–vine   moon–light
some–where   in–to

When your student understands these rules, carefully go over the lesson and listen as he reads the words orally before he does the work by himself.

Page 155

Purpose
To teach the rules about dividing words that have a **suffix** or **prefix**.

Lesson
Review about each syllable having one vowel sound as in **catch, smart, know, swing, etc.**

Talk about words having a suffix such as:

faith–ful   laugh–ing   hope–less

Discuss **Rule Three** about suffixes:

When a word has suffix that makes a vowel sound, divide the word between the root word and the suffix.

Talk about words having a prefix such as:

un–lock   dis–please   fore–arm

Discuss **Rule Four** about prefixes:

When a word has prefix that makes a vowel sound, divide the word between the prefix and the root word.

When your student understands these rules, carefully go over the lesson and listen as he reads the words orally before he does the work by himself.

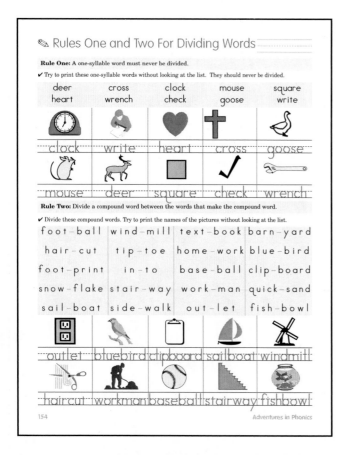

Page 156

Purpose

To review prefixes **un-**, **dis-**, **ex-**, and **re-**.

Lesson

Carefully go over the rules and directions in the lesson. In addition, simply explain that some words have three syllables, as in **dis-o-bey** and **ex-cit-ed**.

Note that the rule for dividing words like *obey* is first stated on page 183 of the workbook; therefore, do not stress this presently. The important concept here is dividing words after prefixes.

When your student understands these rules, listen as he reads the words orally before he does the work by himself.

Page 157

Purpose

1. To review prefixes **pre-**, **fore-**, and **for-**.

2. To teach the prefix **in-**.

Lesson

Carefully go over the rules and directions in the lesson.

When your student understands these rules, listen as he reads the words orally before he does the work by himself.

Remind your student that the letter **a** may take the *schwa* sound, especially at the beginning of a word.

Review of Prefixes ✎ un-, dis-, ex-, and re-

REMEMBER: A **prefix** is a syllable placed at the beginning of a *root* word to change its meaning.
Rule Four: Divide a word with a prefix between the **prefix** and the *root* word.

The prefixes **un-** and **dis-** usually give the *root* word the *opposite* meaning.
The **ex-** usually means *out of* or *from*. The prefix **re-** usually means *do again*.

✔ Divide these words and use the underlined words to complete the sentences below.

dis-o-bey	un-true	re-fill	ex-<u>plore</u>
ex-plode	un-chain	un-safe	ex-pert
<u>un</u>-wrapped	<u>re</u>-read	<u>ex</u>-cit-ed	<u>ex</u>-press
un-pack	dis-trust	un-like	re-wash
<u>re</u>-write	<u>re</u>-ceive	<u>un</u>-load	<u>re</u>-wrap
un-tie	dis-charge	ex-plain	dis-please

1. Ted was happy to <u>receive</u> a letter from his Uncle Jim.

2. Right away he <u>reread</u> the letter to his parents.

3. He was <u>excited</u> that his parents let him go to visit him.

4. Tim wrote a note to his uncle, but he had to <u>rewrite</u> it so it would be neater.

5. Mother had to <u>rewrap</u> Uncle Jim's gift which their baby had <u>unwrapped</u>.

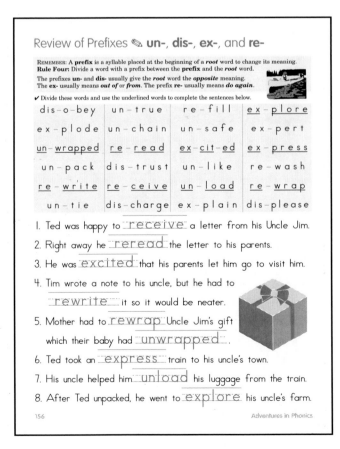

6. Ted took an <u>express</u> train to his uncle's town.

7. His uncle helped him <u>unload</u> his luggage from the train.

8. After Ted unpacked, he went to <u>explore</u> his uncle's farm.

156   Adventures in Phonics

Review of Prefixes ✎ pre-, fore-, and for-

REMEMBER: A **prefix** is a syllable placed at the beginning of a *root* word to change its meaning.
Rule Four: Divide a word with a prefix between the **prefix** and the *root* word.

The prefix **pre-** usually means *before* or *ahead*. The prefix **de-** usually means *from*.
The prefix **fore-** usually means *before in time or place*. **For-** usually means *away*, *apart*, or *off*.

✔ Divide these words and use the underlined words to complete the sentences below.

de-part	pre-dict	de-tour	for-ward
pre-fix	<u>be</u>-<u>cause</u>	de-lay	<u>a</u>-<u>round</u>
<u>pre</u>-pare	de-rail	fore-noon	be-tween
pre-paid	de-frost	<u>for</u>-<u>get</u>	a-gain
<u>pre</u>-<u>vent</u>	<u>a</u>-<u>woke</u>	for-ever	be-came
pre-view	de-press	fore-head	<u>be</u>-<u>fore</u>

1. Pam told Ann a big secret <u>before</u> she went to her home.

2. At night she could not <u>forget</u> about the secret.

3. It would <u>prevent</u> Ann from falling asleep quickly.

4. As Ann <u>awoke</u> in the morning, she became excited again.

5. She went <u>around</u> her room putting her things away.

6. She helped <u>prepare</u> breakfast and told her family the secret.

7. Then she asked if she may be excused <u>because</u> she wanted to run and see Pam's new baby sister.

✔ Add the beginning syllable or prefix **in-** to complete these words. See how quickly you can read them.

<u>in</u>form	<u>in</u>side	<u>in</u>crease	<u>in</u>deed	<u>in</u>stead
<u>in</u>to	<u>in</u>land	<u>in</u>vite	<u>in</u>vent	<u>in</u>dent

Level B   157

Page 158

Purpose

To teach about *accents* in words.

Lesson

Spend enough time on this lesson to help your student understand about accents.

Say these words correctly then incorrectly.

mar' ble	*not*	mar **ble**'
help' ful	*not*	help **ful**'
cloud' y	*not*	cloud **y**'
re **turn**'	*not*	**re**' turn

Carefully go over the rules and directions in the lesson.

When your student understands these rules, listen as he reads the words orally before he does the work by himself.

Page 159

Purpose

To teach about the *schwa* sound made by any of the vowels in the **unaccented** syllable of certain words.

Lesson

Say these words to your student, explaining that the **unaccented** syllable (in these words it is the last syllable, except for the two words that begin with the *schwa* sound of **a**) has the short vowel sound which is like the short **u** sound:

Je' s<u>u</u>s	**bot**' t<u>o</u>m	<u>a</u> **go**'
cam' <u>e</u>l	**man**' n<u>a</u>	<u>a</u> **round**'

Carefully go over the rules and directions in the lesson with your student.

When he has a good understanding, listen as he reads the words orally before he does the work by himself.

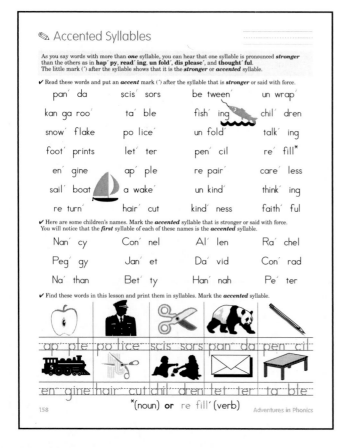

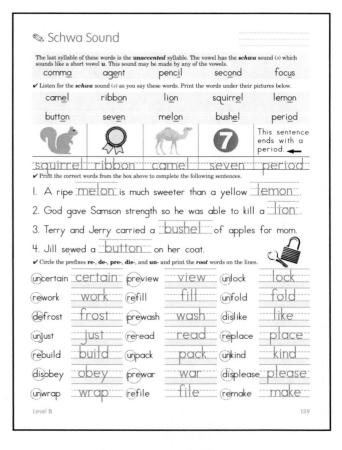

Page 160

Purpose

1. To teach about more words that have the *schwa* sound made by the vowel **a**.

2. To review adding the suffix **y** to short vowel words.

Lesson

Carefully go over the rules and directions in the lesson with your student.

When he has a good understanding, listen as he reads the words orally before he does the work by himself.

Page 161

Purpose

1. To teach about words with the *schwa* sound made by the letters **le**.

2. To teach how words ending with **le** are to be divided.

Lesson

Carefully go over the rules and directions in the lesson with your student.

When he has a good understanding, listen as he reads the words orally before he does the work by himself.

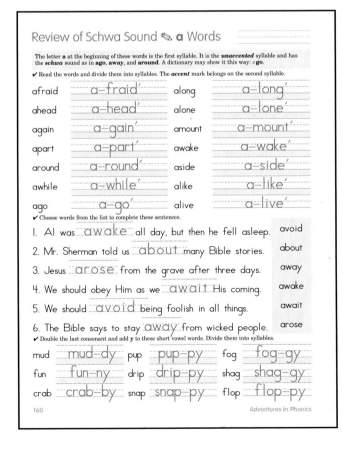

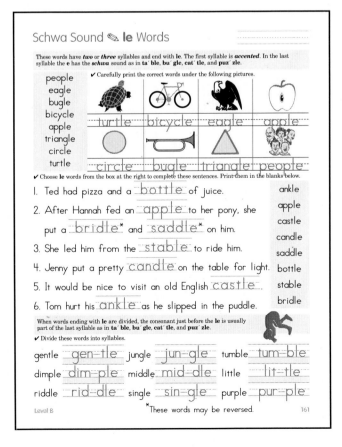

Page 162

Purpose

1. To teach more about words with the *schwa* sound made by the letters **le**.

2. To give more practice in dividing words that end with **le**.

Lesson

Carefully go over the rules and directions in the lesson with your student.

When he has a good understanding, listen as he reads the words orally before he does the work by himself.

Page 163

Purpose

1. To teach about words with the *schwa* sound ending with **ckle**.

2. To teach about dividing words that end with **ckle** or **le**.

Lesson

Print these words on the board/paper or have your student look at this page.

mar-b-le   han-d-le   crum-b-le

Discuss the rule about dividing the word with a consonant staying with the **le**.

Do the same with these words.

pick-le   tack-le   freck-le

Teach the rule that in words ending with **ckle**, the **le** stands alone. The letters **ck** must always be with the short vowel sound.

Carefully go over the rules and directions in the lesson with your student.

When he has a good understanding, listen as he reads the lists of words orally before he does the work by himself.

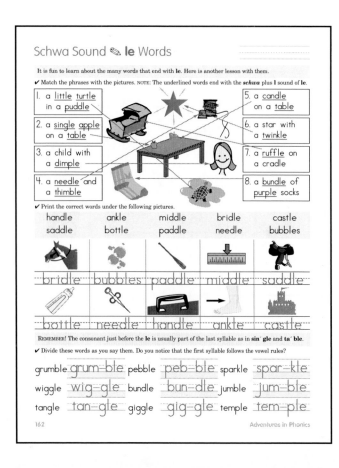

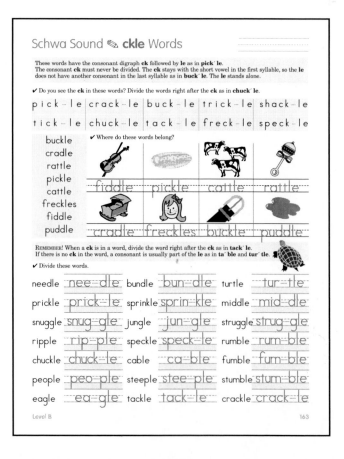

Page 164

Purpose
1. To review several of the sounds made by the vowel **a**.
2. To have additional practice with **le** words

Lesson
Print these sounds and words on the board/paper and talk about the sounds of the vowel **a**. Does your student know and hear these sounds of the **a**?

ă	ā	ə̄ / a
hand	pray	along
tag	train	away
saddle	stable	alike
map	gate	around

After discussing each line, have him mark the **a**.

Carefully go over the rules and directions in the lesson with your student.

In regard to the exercise at the bottom of page 164, explain that the prefix *bi-* means "two," so *bicycle* means "two cycles" (or "two wheels").

When he has a good understanding, listen as he gives the answers orally before he does the work by himself.

Page 165

Purpose
1. To review words with the soft **c** or **g** that end with the silent **e**.
2. To teach that some words ending with the sound of **s**, **r**, or **v** may end with a silent **e**.

Lesson
Review the rules about the letters **c** and **g** having the soft sound when followed by **e**, **i**, or **y** as in the following words:

ice	nice	face	grace
pencil	age	cage	edge
ledge	ginger	cymbal	gym

Explain that some words ending with the sound made by **s**, **r**, or **v** may end with a silent **e** even if the vowel is not a long vowel sound, such as:

have	give	shove	goose
more	love	care	glove

Carefully go over the rules and directions in the lesson with your student.

When he has a good understanding, listen as he gives the answers orally before he does the work by himself.

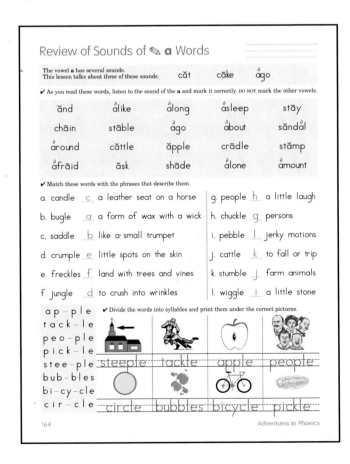

Review of Sounds of ✎ a Words

The vowel **a** has several sounds.
This lesson talks about three of these sounds.   căt   cāke   əgo

✔ As you read these words, listen to the sound of the **a** and mark it correctly. DO NOT mark the other vowels.

ănd	əlike	əlong	ăsleep	stāy
chāin	stāble	əgo	əbout	săndəl
əround	căttle	ăpple	crādle	stămp
əfrāid	ăsk	shāde	əlone	əmount

✔ Match these words with the phrases that describe them.

a. candle __c__ a leather seat on a horse
b. bugle __a__ a form of wax with a wick
c. saddle __b__ like a small trumpet
d. crumple __e__ little spots on the skin
e. freckles __f__ land with trees and vines
f. jungle __d__ to crush into wrinkles
g. people __h__ a little laugh
h. chuckle __g__ persons
i. pebble __l__ jerky motions
j. cattle __k__ to fall or trip
k. stumble __j__ farm animals
l. wiggle __i__ a little stone

ap-ple
tack-le
peo-ple
pick-le
stee-ple   steeple   tackle   apple   people
bub-bles
bi-cy-cle
cir-cle   circle   bubbles   bicycle   pickle

✔ Divide the words into syllables and print them under the correct pictures.

164   Adventures in Phonics

Words Ending with Silent ✎ e

These words end with the vowel **e**. Words ending with soft **c** (*s*) or **g** (*j*), usually have a final silent **e**. Usually a silent **e** follows words ending with the letters **s**, **r**, or **v**.

✔ Read the following words with a silent **e** and print them under the correct pictures.

nurse	geese	fence	bounce	hinge
store	blouse	purse	mouse	glove

glove   blouse   nurse   hinge   geese

fence   store   bounce   purse   mouse

✔ Read the following words with a silent **e** and print them in the correct blanks below.

plunge	loose	more	have
choice	ounce	since	give

1. The ring felt light __since__ it weighed only one __ounce__.
2. We saw the man __plunge__ into the lake to save the child.
3. Our teacher will __give__ us a __choice__ of books to read.
4. Ed's shoes were __loose__, so he tied the laces once __more__.
5. We __have__ many wonderful ways to serve our great Lord.

✔ Add the suffix **-ing** to these words which end with a silent **e** by dropping the **e** and adding **ing**.

serve __serving__ plunge __plunging__ have __having__
bounce __bouncing__ give __giving__ store __storing__

Level B   165

Page 166

Purpose

1. To review that the vowels **i** and **o** may sometimes have the long vowel sound even when they are the only vowel in the word.

2. To teach about adding the suffix **-ing** to words ending with **w**, **x**, or **y**.

Lesson

Review the rule that a single **i** usually is short, except when it is followed by **ld**, **nd**, or **gh**. The **gh** is silent.

child   mild   find   kind   right

Also review the rule that a single **o** usually has the short sound, but may have the long vowel sound when followed by two consonants such as **ld**, **st**, **th**, **ll**, and **lt**.

cold   most   both   stoll   colt

Carefully discuss the rule about adding the suffix **-ing** to words ending with **w**, **x**, or **y**.

bowing   taxing   crying   playing

When your student seems to understand the lesson, listen as he gives the answers orally before he does the work by himself.

Page 167

Purpose

1. To review the **ûr** sound made with sets of letters **er**, **ir**, **ur**, **ear**, and **(w)or**.

2. To review the rule about doubling the last consonant of a short vowel word when adding a suffix beginning with a vowel such as in **-ing**.

Lesson

Reading the words on Charts 32 and 33 (page 225 in the workbook) would be good drill for reviewing the modified **er** sound.

When your student seems to understand the lesson, listen as he gives the answers orally before he does the work by himself.

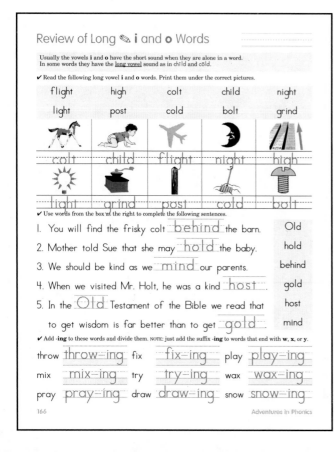

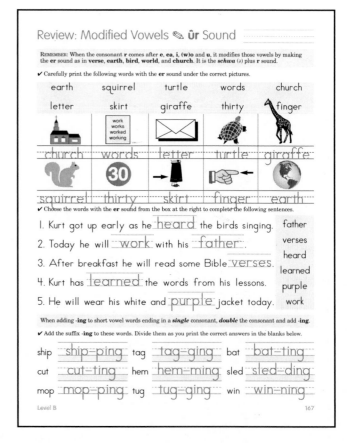

Page 168

Purpose
1. To review the three sounds made by the letters **ear: ear** as in **dear**, **ear** as in **earth**, and **ear** as in **pear**.
2. To review the rule about adding **-es** when making words that end with **s, x, z, ch,** or **sh** plural.

Lesson
Ask your student to say these sounds and words:

ē ̯r	e ̯r	̯âr
dear	earn	bear
fear	earth	pear
gear	learn	tear
hear	pearl	wear
near	search	swear

Review the rule about adding **-es** to make words that end with **s, x, z, ch,** or **sh** plural. (*See page 134 in the workbook.*)

When the student understands the page and has given the answers orally, have him do the work by himself.

Page 169

Purpose
To review the three sounds made by the vowels **ea**.

Lesson
Ask your student to say these sounds and words:

ē ̯	̯ā	ĕ ̯
deal	break	bread
flea	great	deaf
leap	steak	head
meal	breaking	health
sea	greater	meant

When he understands the page and has given the answers orally, have him do the work by himself.

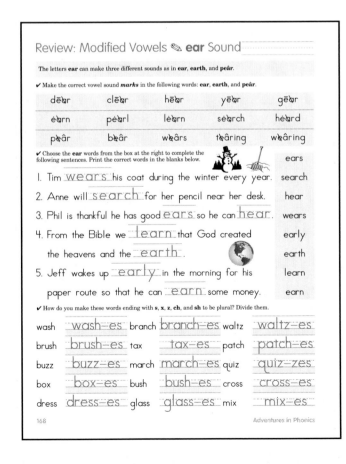

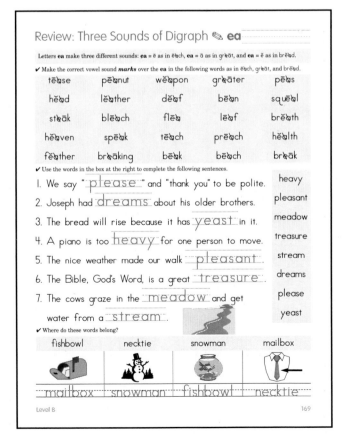

Page 170

Purpose
To review words ending with the long vowel sound.

Lesson
Talk about the long vowel sound that is made by one vowel at the end of these words:

o	e	i*	y
go	be	hi	cry
lo	he	hi-fi	dry
ho	me	pi	fry
no	she	chi	shy
so	we		try

* Note that the long **i** words are not required, but the student should be aware of them. The words *pi* (π) and *chi* (χ) are names for letters from the Greek alphabet and are used in mathematical equations.

Listen as your student reads the long vowel words in Chart 20 (page 221 in the workbook), and discuss the exceptions to the rule.

When your student understands the page and has given the answers orally, have him do the work independently.

Page 171

Purpose
To teach words with **ie** making the long vowel **e** sound.

Lesson
Talk about the vowels **ie** sometimes making the long vowel **e** sound,. and ask your student to read these words:

chief	relief	pier
thief	field	shriek
grief	yield	fierce
brief	shield	pierce
belief	priest	niece

When your student understands the page and has given the answers orally, have him do the work independently.

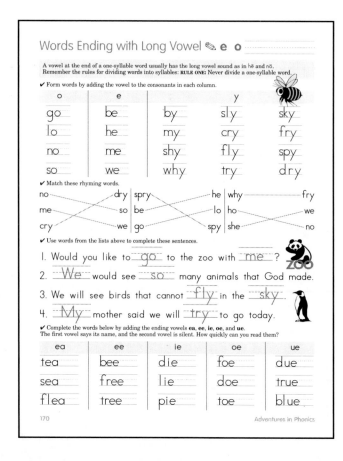

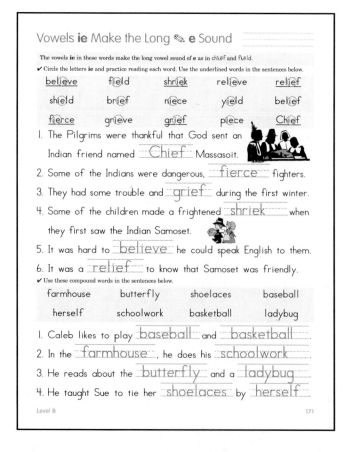

Page 172

Purpose
To review words with the sound of ô made by the letters **o** or **al**.

Lesson
It would be a good drill for your student to read the words in the first five columns of Chart 35 (page 226 in the workbook).

When he understands the page and has given the answers orally, have him do the work independently.

Page 173

Purpose
To review words with the sound of ô made by the letters **aw**, **ough**, and **augh**.

Lesson
Listen to your student read the words in Chart 36.

When he understands the page and has given the answers orally, have him do the work independently.

Review of ✎ ô Words

Do you remember the different sounds that the vowel **o** has?

o as in **ox**   ŏ as in **o̅o̅k**   o̅o̅ as in **spo̅o̅n**   o̅o̅ as in **bo̅o̅k**   ô as in **crôss**   ŭ as in **son**

✔ Match these words with their meanings. Use the underlined words in the following sentences.

1. gloss	3 angry		1. lost	2 frozen dew	
2. toss	2 throw		2. frost	3 the price	
3. cross	4 green plant		3. cost	4 not on	
4. moss	1 shine		4. off	1 not found	

1. log	4 a large pig		1. moth	4 not hard	
2. fog	3 hopping animal		2. broth	1 an insect	
3. frog	2 clouds near land		3. cloth	3 used for clothes	
4. hog	1 part of tree		4. soft	2 thin soup	

1. Al sees a __frog__ on a log that is covered with __moss__.

2. He put a brown __cloth__ that is __soft__ over the frog.

3. He will try to catch it before it jumps __off__ of the __log__.

When the vowel **a** is followed by an **l**, it usually has the ô sound. as in **hall**, **walk**, and **salt**.

✔ Match these words with their meanings.

1. all	4 little		1. walk	2 a plant stem	
2. halt	3 tumble over		2. stalk	3 a passageway	
3. fall	2 stop		3. hall	4 speak or yell	
4. small	1 everything		4. call	1 move on foot	

172   Adventures in Phonics

Review of ✎ ô Words

The sound of **ô** is often made with the letters **aw** as in **law** and **claw**.

✔ Match these words with their meanings.

1. jaw	4 chews		1. hawk	4 begins to melt	
2. paw	1 part of mouth		2. dawn	3 grassy yard	
3. straw	2 animal's foot		3. lawn	1 large bird	
4. gnaws	3 dried grain stalk		4. thaws	2 early morning	

1. crawl	4 terrible		1. awning	3 not cooked	
2. claw	3 young deer		2. yawn	4 cutting tool	
3. fawn	2 bird's sharp nail		3. raw	1 cover for shade	
4. awful	1 move like baby		4. saw	2 deep breath	

The sound of **ô** may also be spelled with the letters **ough** as in **bought** and **augh** as in **caught**.

✔ Print these words next to their meanings. Use the underlined words in the sentences below.

__taught__   caught   __daughter__   brought   __thought__   naughty   __bought__   ought

did teach	taught	did think	thought
a parents' girl	daughter	to not behave	naughty
did catch	caught	did buy	bought
did bring	brought	should	ought

1. Mrs. Smith __bought__ a toy bear for her __daughter__.

2. Anne __thought__ that it was tired and ought to sleep.

3. Her mother __taught__ her how to sew a blanket.

Level B   173

Page 174

Purpose
To review words with the sound of ô made with the letters **ough** or **augh**.

Lesson
Can your student quickly read the words in the last two columns of Chart 36 (page 226 in the workbook)? If not, it would be good to have him read them several times.

When he understands the page and has given the answers orally, have him do the work independently.

Page 175

Purpose
To review more words with the sound of ô made by **al** and **aw**.

Lesson
Can your student quickly read the words in the fourth and fifth columns of Chart 35, and the first four columns of Chart 36? If not, have him read them several times.

When he understands the page and has given the answers orally, have him do the work independently.

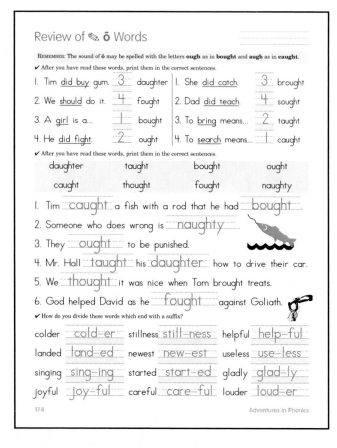

Page 176

Purpose

1. To review words with the long **u** vowel sound made with the letters **ew**.

2. To review the rule about adding **-es** when making words that end with **s**, **x**, **z**, **ch**, or **sh** plural.

Lesson

Listen to your student read the words in the last three columns of Chart 19 (page 221 in the workbook).

When he understands the page and has given the answers orally, have him do the work independently.

Page 177

Purpose

1. To review **âr** words made with the letters **air**.

2. To review rules about dividing short vowel words having the suffix **-ing**.

Lesson

Ask your student to read these words:

air   pair   hair   fair   stair

Carefully review this rule:

When a **short vowel word** ends with a single consonant, that consonant is usually doubled before adding a suffix which begins with a vowel.

hop ⇒ hop|ping   win ⇒ win|ning

These words should be divided right after the root word, which is between the double letters.

You know that many short vowel words end with the double letters: **ff**, **ll**, **ss**, and **zz**

These words should be divided after those double letters.

puff|ing   fill|ing   miss|ing buzz|ing

After answering orally, your student should be ready to do the work by himself.

Review Lesson of ✎ ew Words

Words ending with the long vowel **u** sound often end with the spelling **ew**. The *w* is used as a vowel.

✔ Match these words with their meanings. Use the underlined words to complete the sentences below.

| drew | knew | threw | flew | hew | pew | brew |
| crew | grew | blew | chew | new | stew | dew |

group of workers	crew	thick soup	stew
did draw	drew	water on lawn	dew
eat with teeth	chew	did fly	flew
wind that moved	blew	row of seats	pew
did grow	grew	to carve or cut	hew
did throw	threw	prepare tea	brew
did know	knew	not old	new

1. The boys sat quietly in the first pew of their new church.

2. They had seen the crew of men working hard to build it.

3. They knew they should be quiet and listen each time they come to worship the Lord.

4. If the wind blew, it would strew papers around.

5. The bird flew down to drink some dew on the grass.

✔ Add **-es** to make the following words *plural*. NOTE: These words end with **sh**, **ch**, **s**, **x**, or **z**.

| churches | dishes | brushes | lunches |
| buses | crosses | patches | boxes |

Review Lesson of ✎ âr Words

Words that have the letters **air** make the sound of **âr** as in **stair**.

✔ Print the correct **air** words under their pictures. Use the underlined words in the sentences below.

| hair | airmail | chair | repair | airfield |
| pair | stairway | dairy | fair | airliner |

airliner   chair   pair   hair   stairway

1. Jane saw the crew quickly repair the tire on the airplane.

2. We sent letters airmail to children in Russia.

3. Our class enjoyed the field trip to the dairy farm.

REMEMBER: When a short vowel word ends in a *single* consonant, that consonant is usually *doubled* before adding a suffix which begins with a vowel as in **cut** ⇒ **cutting** and **hop** ⇒ **hopping**.

✔ Underline the *root* words as they were before **-ing** was added. Divide the words into syllables. BE CAREFUL! If the *root* words end with ll, ss, ff, or zz, DO NOT divide those double letters.

tap - ping	tip - ping	puff - ing	hop - ping
will - ing	jump - ing	chop - ping	fluff - ing
read - ing	hit - ting	fuss - ing	roll - ing
buzz - ing	fill - ing	win - ning	sun - ning

✔ The letter **e** was taken off before adding the suffix **-ing**. Write the *root* words of these words.

making	make	baking	bake	poking	poke
coming	come	sharing	share	taming	tame
giving	give	wasting	waste	piling	pile

Page 178

Purpose

1. To review words with the soft sound **c**.

2. To have additional practice in adding suffixes **-er** and **-est** to words.

Lesson

Listen to your student read the words on Chart 37 (page 227 in the workbook).

Review the rule about doubling the single consonant in a short vowel word before adding a suffix that begins with a vowel.

sad   sad-der   sad-dest

When your student understands the page and has given the answers orally, have him do the work independently.

Page 179

Purpose

1. To review words with the soft sound **c**.

2. To have additional practice in dividing words into syllables.

Lesson

Listen to your student read the words on Chart 37.

Talk about how a word with a prefix should be divided.

fore–noon   dis–miss   re–plant

When your student understands the page and has given the answers orally, have him do the work independently.

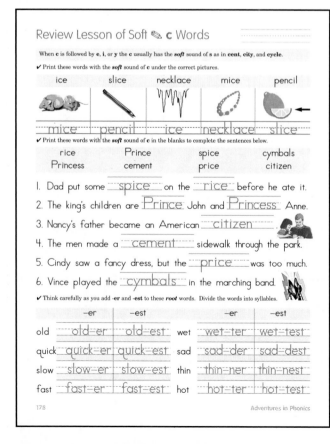

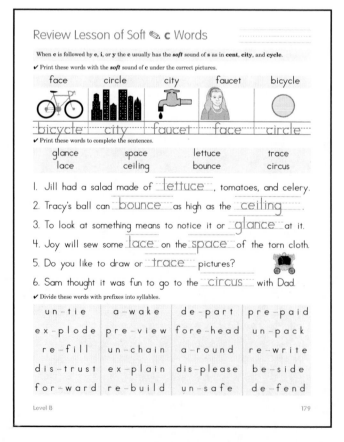

Page 180

Purpose

To learn about **Rule Five** for dividing words into syllables.

Lesson

Discuss **Rule Five:**

> When two or more consonants come between two vowels, the word is usually divided between the first two consonants.

This is an easy rule to learn.

yel–low fin–ger par–rot tur–key

When your student understands the page and has given the answers orally, have him do the work independently.

Page 181

Purpose

To review the **Five Rules** about dividing words into syllables.

Lesson

Carefully discuss each rule with your student.

When he understands the page and has given the answers orally, have him do the work by himself.

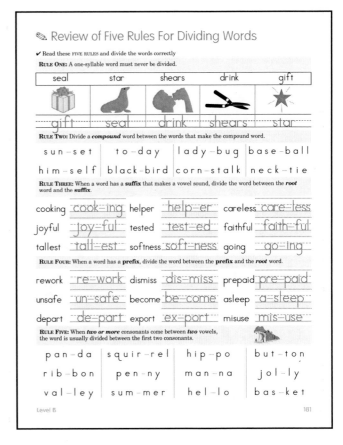

Page 182

Purpose

To learn about **Rule Six** for dividing words into syllables. To review the rule about dividing words ending with **le** or **ckle**.

Lesson

Discuss **Rule Six**:

When a single consonant comes between two vowels, the word is usually divided *after the consonant* if the *first* vowel sound is **short**.

shad–ow   heav–en   sev–en

As is true about many rules, we need to listen to the vowel sound. This rule may remind us of short vowel words that end with a consonant.

cab–in   chap–el   fig–ure

Review the rule about dividing words ending with **le** or **ckle**.

cir–cle   rum–ble   bot–tle
pick–le   tack–le   buck–le

When your student understands the page and has given the answers orally, have him do the work independently.

Page 183

Purpose

To learn about **Rule Seven** for dividing words into syllables. To review the suffix -er.

Lesson

Discuss **Rule Seven**:

When a single consonant comes between two vowels, the word is usually divided *before the consonant* if the *first* vowel sound is **long**.

pa–per   se–cret   mu–sic

Again it is important to listen to vowel sounds! This rule reminds us of words that end with a long vowel sound.

no–tice   go–pher   so–lo
free–dom   He–brew   lo–cal

Talk about how the suffix -er changes or modifies a word such as in:

speak ⇒ **speak**′ er
point ⇒ **point**′ er

When your student understands the page and has given the answers orally, have him do the work independently.

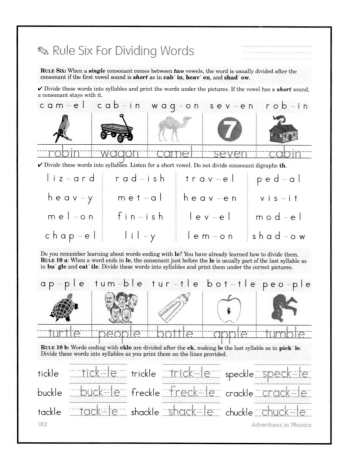

✎ Rule Six For Dividing Words

RULE SIX: When a *single* consonant comes between *two* vowels, the word is usually divided after the consonant if the first vowel sound is *short* as in **cab´ in, heav´ en,** and **shad´ ow.**

✔ Divide these words into syllables and print the words under the pictures. If the vowel has a *short* sound, a consonant stays with it.

cam–el   cab–in   wag–on   sev–en   rob–in

robin   wagon   camel   seven   cabin

✔ Divide these words into syllables. Listen for a short vowel. Do not divide consonant digraphs th.

liz–ard	rad–ish	trav–el	ped–al
heav–y	met–al	heav–en	vis–it
mel–on	fin–ish	lev–el	mod–el
chap–el	lil–y	lem–on	shad–ow

Do you remember learning about words ending with **le**? You have already learned how to divide them.
RULE 10 a: When a word ends in **le**, the consonant just before the **le** is usually part of the last syllable as in **bu´ gle** and **cat´ tle**. Divide these words into syllables and print them under the correct pictures.

ap–ple   tum–ble   tur–tle   bot–tle   peo–ple

turtle   people   bottle   apple   tumble

RULE 10 b: Words ending with **ckle** are divided after the **ck**, making **le** the last syllable as in **pick´ le**. Divide these words into syllables as you print them on the lines provided.

tickle	tick–le	trickle	trick–le	speckle	speck–le
buckle	buck–le	freckle	freck–le	crackle	crack–le
tackle	tack–le	shackle	shack–le	chuckle	chuck–le

182   Adventures in Phonics

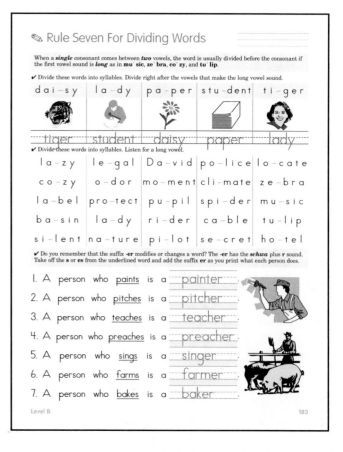

✎ Rule Seven For Dividing Words

When a *single* consonant comes between *two* vowels, the word is usually divided before the consonant if the first vowel sound is *long* as in **mu´ sic, ze´ bra, co´ zy,** and **tu´ lip.**

✔ Divide these words into syllables. Divide right after the vowels that make the long vowel sound.

dai–sy   la–dy   pa–per   stu–dent   ti–ger

tiger   student   daisy   paper   lady

✔ Divide these words into syllables. Listen for a long vowel.

la–zy	le–gal	Da–vid	po–lice	lo–cate
co–zy	o–dor	mo–ment	cli–mate	ze–bra
la–bel	pro–tect	pu–pil	spi–der	mu–sic
ba–sin	la–dy	ri–der	ca–ble	tu–lip
si–lent	na–ture	pi–lot	se–cret	ho–tel

✔ Do you remember that the suffix **-er** modifies or changes a word? The **-er** has the *schwa* plus r sound. Take off the **s** or **es** from the underlined word and add the suffix **er** as you print what each person does.

1. A person who underline{paints} is a   painter
2. A person who underline{pitches} is a   pitcher
3. A person who underline{teaches} is a   teacher
4. A person who underline{preaches} is a   preacher
5. A person who underline{sings} is a   singer
6. A person who underline{farms} is a   farmer
7. A person who underline{bakes} is a   baker

Level B   183

Page 184

Purpose

1. To learn that the letters **ei** usually make the long **a** sound.

2. To learn the rule about adding the suffix **-er** to words ending with a **y**.

Lesson

Teach your students that the letters **eigh** make the long vowel **a** sound. The letters **ey** may also make the long vowel **a** sound. Have them read all of the words on Chart 40 (page 228 in the workbook) until they can say them quickly.

Discuss this rule:

> When a word ends with a consonant and **y**, change the **y** to **i** when you need to add the suffixes **-er** or **-est**.

> happy   happier   happiest

When your student understands the page and has given the answers orally, have him do the work independently.

Page 185

Purpose

1. To review words with the consonant digraphs **kn** and **wr**.

2. To review words with the vowels **ei** having the long **a** vowel sound.

3. To review words with the **eâr** sound.

Lesson

Listen to your student read the words in Chart 42 (page 228 in the workbook), as well as the words on Chart 40.

When your student understands the page and has given the answers orally, have him do the work independently.

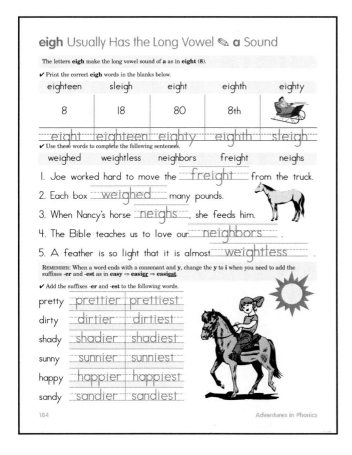

Page 186

Purpose
To work with words having the soft sound of **g**.

Lesson
Listen to your student read the words on Chart 38 (page 227 in the workbook).

Give special attention to the vowel sounds in these words with **dge** and **ge** or **nge**.

Usually the vowel is <u>short</u> before the letters **dge**.

b r i d g e　　　b a d g e　　　p l e d g e

Usually the vowel is <u>long</u> before the letters **ge** or **nge**.

c a g e　　　s t a g e　　　m a n g e r

When your student has carefully gone over the page with you and has given the answers orally, have him do the work independently.

Page 187

Purpose
1. To teach how to change words ending with **f** or **fe** to be *plural*.

2. To review the rules for making other words plural.

Lesson
Discuss this rule about how to change words ending with **f** or **fe** to become *plural*:

When a word ends with **f** or **fe**, change the **f** or **fe** to **v** and add the suffix **-es** to make the word plural.

Show these examples:

wolf ⇒ wolves　　　life ⇒ lives
loaf ⇒ loaves　　　knife ⇒ knives

Carefully review the rules in the center of the lesson.

When your student has carefully gone over the page with you and has given the answers orally, have him do the work independently.

Review Lesson of Soft g Words

When **g** is followed by **e, i,** or **y,** the **g** usually has the *soft* sound of **j** as in **cage, giant,** and **gym.** Some exceptions to this rule are as follows: **get, gift,** and **give.**

✔ Print the correct words with the *soft* sound of **g** under their pictures.

cage	pledge	orange	bridge	pigeon
wedge	giraffe	engine	badge	hinge
pledge	engine	bridge	wedge	giraffe
pigeon	orange	cage	hinge	badge

✔ Choose the correct words to complete the following sentences. Print them in the blanks below.

Judge	danger	village	manger	Egypt

1. Jesus Christ was born in the little **village** of Bethlehem.
2. Mary laid Him in a **manger** because there was no bed.
3. Jesus was in **danger** of being killed by evil King Herod.
4. God told Joseph to take Him to safety in **Egypt**.
5. Jesus Christ is our Creator, Saviour, King, and **Judge**.

A vowel before the letters **dge** usually has the *short* sound as in **bridge** and **wedge**.
A vowel before the letters **ge** or **nge** usually has the *long* sound as in **cage** and **manger**.

✔ Print the *first* vowel on the line and mark it to show if it has a *short* or *long* sound.

age ā　badge ă　stage ā　budge ŭ　dodge ŏ
danger ā　ridge ĭ　huge ū　page ā　angel ā

Making Plural Words Ending in f or fe

When a word ends in **f** or **fe,** change the **f** or **fe** to **v** and add the suffix **-es** to make the word *plural* as in **calf** ⇒ **calves** and **knife** ⇒ **knives.** Two exceptions are as follows: **belief** ⇒ **beliefs** and **chief** ⇒ **chiefs.**

✔ Use the RULE above to make the following **f** and **fe** words *plural*, except for **chief.**

leaf	leaves	wife	wives		
calf	calves	scarf	scarves	loaf	loaves
wolf	wolves	half	halves	knife	knives
shelf	shelves	chief	chiefs	life	lives

✔ Print the singular *root* words for these *plural* words.

wolves	wolf	thieves	thief	knives	knife
lives	life	shelves	shelf	leaves	leaf
loaves	loaf	calves	calf	wives	wife

Do you remember? Often we just add an **-s** to make words *plural*.
1. If a word ends with **y** and a vowel is right before it, just add **-s** as in **boys** and **monkeys.**
2. Change the **y** to **i** and add **-es** when the **y** comes after a consonant as in **babies** and **ladies.**
3. If a word ends with **s, x, z, sh,** or **ch,** add **-es** as in **buses, boxes, buzzes, dishes,** and **lunches.**

✔ Make the following words *plural*.

valley	valleys	turkey	turkeys		
fly	flies	box	boxes	church	churches
brush	brushes	bench	benches	tax	taxes
pencil	pencils	dress	dresses	pony	ponies
city	cities	beach	beaches	lily	lilies
joy	joys	lady	ladies	ranch	ranches
splash	splashes	table	tables	ax	axes

Page 188

Purpose

1. To teach one of the purposes for an **apostrophe**.

2. To review the rule for changing words ending with **f** or **fe** to become plural.

Lesson

Using the rule at the top of the lesson, explain how the apostrophe helps to show ownership. Perhaps use your student's name for an example.

book of Kelsey ⇒ Kelsey's book

paw of dog ⇒ dog's paw

dress of sister ⇒ sister's dress

When you have carefully gone over the page with your student and he has given the answers orally, have him do the work independently.

Page 189

Purpose

1. To review **Rules Six** and **Seven** about dividing words into syllables.

2. To review the use of the apostrophe to show ownership.

Lesson

Remind the student to listen to the first vowel sound in the words. This will help him to divide correctly.

Using the rules as they are written at the top of the lesson, go over the words in the exercises below for examples.

When you have carefully gone over the page with your student and he has given the answers orally, have him do the work independently.

The Apostrophe ✎ ' For Possession

The little mark called the *apostrophe* (') is used in a two of ways. The first way is as follows:
RULE 1: To show that someone or something owns or possesses something, usually an *apostrophe* and an **s** (**'s**) are added to the end of the word. (**RULE 2**, concerning contractions, is covered in a later lesson.)
the cat's dish   the lady's purse   the man's hat   a friend's home   Dan's car.

✔ Add an *apostrophe* and an **s** (**'s**) to show possession or ownership.

jacket of Luke	Luke's jacket	dog of John	John's dog
coat of Anna	Anna's coat	shoe of Jay	Jay's shoe
book of Greg	Greg's book	dress of Ruth	Ruth's dress
doll of Jessica	Jessica's doll	truck of Ben	Ben's truck
desk of Levi	Levi's desk	Bible of Paul	Paul's Bible

✔ Add an *apostrophe* and an **s** (**'s**) to show possession or ownership as you complete these sentences.

1. Grace gave Janelle a pencil, so it is   Janelle's pencil
2. If Connel owns a sailboat, it is   Connel's sailboat.
3. Her father gave Kelsey a gift, so it is   Kelsey's gift
4. Eric was given a rabbit, so it is   Eric's rabbit
5. Because God created our world, it is   God's world
6. If a pen belongs to Mr. Sherman, it is   Mr. Sherman's pen.
7. Hannah owns scissors, so they are   Hannah's scissors.

✔ Make these words *plural* by changing the **f** or **fe** to **v** and adding **-es**, except for **belief**.

leaf	leaves	wolf	wolves	scarf	scarves	half	halves
life	lives	shelf	shelves	knife	knives	thief	thieves
calf	calves	loaf	loaves	belief	beliefs	wife	wives

Syllables ✎ Rules Six and Seven

RULE SIX: When a *single* consonant comes between *two* vowels, the word is usually divided after the consonant if the first vowel sound is **short** as in cab' in, heav' en, and moth' er. The short vowel needs a consonant.

RULE SEVEN: When a *single* consonant comes between *two* vowels, the word is usually divided before the consonant if the first vowel sound is **long** as in mu' sic, ze' bra, and co' zy. The long vowel can stand alone.

✔ Divide these words according to the RULES above.

finish	fin-ish	heavy	heav-y		
robin	rob-in	cover	cov-er	tiger	ti-ger
radish	rad-ish	metal	met-al	tulip	tu-lip
cabin	cab-in	legal	le-gal	pony	po-ny
chapel	chap-el	story	sto-ry	label	la-bel
wagon	wag-on	paper	pa-per	cozy	co-zy
river	riv-er	lazy	la-zy	motor	mo-tor

✔ Think carefully of the RULES as you listen to the first vowels, and then divide the words.

lady	la-dy	seven	sev-en	⑦	
travel	trav-el	regal	re-gal	zebra	ze-bra
petal	pet-al	quiver	quiv-er	model	mod-el

✔ Do you remember how to use an *apostrophe* and **s**? The **cap** that belongs to **Sam** is written: **Sam's cap.**

1. When William eats an apple, is it   William's apple
2. If a kangaroo has food, it is the   kangaroo's food.
3. If a squirrel found a nut, it is the   squirrel's nut
4. Tom got a letter in the mail, so it is   Tom's letter

Page 190

Purpose
To teach the second purpose for an **apostrophe**.

Lesson
Using the rule at the top of the lesson, explain how the apostrophe helps make two special words into one word. Go over this lesson carefully for good understanding.

When you have carefully gone over the page with your student and he has given the answers orally, he may then print the answers independently.

Page 191

Purpose
To teach that the letter **s** may sometimes have the sound of **z**.

To apply both rules of the **apostrophe**.

Lesson
Listen closely as your student says the words in the first exercise to you. There may be a few words that could have either the **s** or **z** sound.

Review each apostrophe rule as well as the exercises below them.

When you have carefully gone over the page with your student and he has given the answers orally, he may then print the answers independently.

The Apostrophe ✎ ' With Contractions

A **contraction** is a short way of writing two words. They are written together, but **one or more** letters are left out. This lesson gives the second way in which the **apostrophe** is used.
RULE 2: An **apostrophe** is used to replace the missing letters. Usually the first word is not changed.

do not ⇒ don't   they will ⇒ they'll   he is ⇒ he's   you are ⇒ you're

✔ Write these words as **contractions**. Take out the underlined letters as in **do not ⇒ don't**.

do not	don't	he will	he'll	he is	he's
has not	hasn't	she will	she'll	she is	she's
have not	haven't	we will	we'll	it is	it's
should not	shouldn't	they will	they'll	here is	here's
were not	weren't	it will	it'll	we are	we're
was not	wasn't	you will	you'll	they are	they're

✔ Write the words below the blanks as **contractions**. Take out the underlined letters as in **is not ⇒ isn't**.

1. Jim wasn't in school today, because he didn't feel well.
   (was not)   (did not)

2. Jesse couldn't reach the top shelf; he isn't tall enough.
   (could not)   (is not)

3. We'll go to lunch as soon as we're finished with math.
   (We will)   (we are)

4. Angela isn't sure that she'll be able to eat all her pizza.
   (is not)   (she will)

✔ See how nicely you can draw pictures of these words ending with **le**.

| turtle | candle | bubbles | table | apple |

190   Adventures in Phonics

The Sound of **z** Made by ✎ **s**

Sometimes an **s** can sound like a **z** as in **rose** and **teams**.

✔ Print **s** or **z** on the lines to show the sound made by the **s**.

mouse	s	peels	s or z	gates	s	needless	s
obeys	z	six	s	has	z	wheels	z
horse	s	arise	z	nose	z	rains	s or z

Apostrophe RULE 1: To show that someone or something owns or possesses something, usually an **apostrophe** and an **s** ('s) are added to the end of the word as in **Charles Spurgeon's** son.

✔ Add **'s** to the underlined words to show ownership, and print the phrases to complete the sentences.

1. The white hat on Naomi is   Naomi's hat
2. The bow on the bear is the   bear's bow
3. The dress on the bunny is the   bunny's dress
4. The sail on the boat is the   boat's sail
5. The shirt belongs to Jay; it is   Jay's shirt
6. The pen belongs to Jill; it is   Jill's pen

Apostrophe RULE 2: An **apostrophe** is put in the place of the missing letters which are removed when forming a **contraction**. Usually the first word is not changed.
Contractions can also be written with the word **have** as in **we have ⇒ we've**.

✔ Print these words as **contractions** by taking out the underlined letters and adding an **apostrophe**.

we have	we've	has not	hasn't	you have	you've
would not	wouldn't	they have	they've	let us	let's
we are	we're	she is	she's	he is	he's
they are	they're	should not	shouldn't	could not	couldn't

Level B   191

Page 192

Purpose

To teach additional ways to form some words to be plural.

To review rules for making words *plural*.

Lesson

Have your student read these words with you, explaining that these words need to be changed in this way to become plural.

man	men	goose	geese
woman	women	foot	feet
mouse	mice	tooth	teeth

Carefully review the rules for making words to be plural. After you have listened to your student answer the lesson, ask him to print the lesson independently.

Page 193

Purpose

To give additional practice in changing words to be plural.

Lesson

Carefully review the rules for making words plural, using the words in the list to apply the rules.

After you have gone over the entire lesson and have heard your student give the answers orally, have him complete the page independently.

✎ More Plural Forms of Words

Some words form their *plurals* in an unusual way as in **ox** ⇒ **oxen** and **mouse** ⇒ **mice**.

✔ Print these *plural* words where they belong. Use these words to complete the sentences below.

feet	children	women	teeth	men	geese

tooth	teeth	foot	feet	woman	women
child	children	man	men	goose	geese

1. As the __children__ smiled, their missing __teeth__ showed.

2. The __women__ screamed when they saw the two mice.

3. The __men__ chased the two noisy __geese__ into the barn.

4. The baby's __feet__ were perfectly formed by our Creator.

REMEMBER the following RULES for making words *plural*:
1. To make many words *plural*, just add **-s** as in **cats**.
2. To make words *plural* that end with **sh, ch, s, x,** or **z**, add **-es** as in **dishes**.
3. To make words *plural* that end with **y** follow the next two RULES:
   a. Add **-s** if **y** comes after a vowel as in **boys**.
   b. Change the **y** to **i**, and add **-es**, if **y** comes after a consonant as in **city** ⇒ **cities**.

✔ Think of the above RULES as you make these words plural.

peach	peaches	toy	toys	turkey	turkeys
frog	frogs	box	boxes	fly	flies
sky	skies	jacket	jackets	injury	injuries
girl	girls	tax	taxes	valley	valleys
tray	trays	waltz	waltzes	watch	watches
glass	glasses	bush	bushes	ash	ashes
patch	patches	berry	berries	ox	axes

192   Adventures in Phonics

✎ Review of Plural Words

When a word ends in **f** or **fe**, change the **f** or **fe** to **v** and add the suffix **-es** to make the word *plural* as in **calf** ⇒ **calves** and **knife** ⇒ **knives**. Two exceptions are: **belief** ⇒ **beliefs** and **chief** ⇒ **chiefs**.

✔ Think of the above RULES as you make these words plural.

belief	beliefs	scarf	scarves	wolf	wolves
calf	calves	half	halves	knife	knives
life	lives	loaf	loaves	leaf	leaves
thief	thieves	chief	chiefs	shelf	shelves

REMEMBER the following RULES for making words *plural*:
1. To make many words *plural*, just add **-s** as in **cats**.
2. To make words *plural* that end with **sh, ch, s, x,** or **z**, add **-es** as in **dishes**.
3. To make words *plural* that end with **y** follow the next two RULES:
   a. Add **-s** if **y** comes after a vowel as in **boys**.
   b. Change the **y** to **i**, and add **-es**, if **y** comes after a consonant as in **city** ⇒ **cities**.

✔ Think of the above RULES as you make these words plural.

church	churches	table	tables	brush	brushes
fox	foxes	dress	dresses	boy	boys
turkey	turkeys	lunch	lunches	fly	flies
match	matches	box	boxes	city	cities
girl	girls	cherry	cherries	valley	valleys
tray	trays	track	tracks	tax	taxes

A few words become *plural* in special ways as in **man** ⇒ **men**.

✔ Match the following words to their unusual *plurals*.

man	women	child	mice	goose	workmen
tooth	teeth	mouse	feet	ox	geese
woman	men	foot	children	workman	oxen

Level B   193

Page 194

Purpose

To teach **Rule Eight** about dividing words into syllables.

Lesson

Discuss **Rule Eight** with your student:

> If a vowel is sounded alone in a word, it forms a syllable by itself.

This is not a difficult rule to learn, but you should give as much help as needed to teach a clear understanding of dividing the syllables.

> a–long   a–way   i–dol
>
> o–pen   o–cean   mel–o–dy

Use the list of words in the lesson for examples.

When you have carefully gone over the page with your student and he has given the answers orally, he may then print the answers independently.

Page 195

Purpose

To teach **Rule Nine** about dividing words into syllables.

Lesson

Discuss **Rule Nine** with your student:

> When two vowel come together and are sounded separately, divide the word between the two vowels.

> po–em   u–su–al   cre–ate
>
> sci–ence   li–on   ro–de–o

Use the list of words in the lesson for examples.

When you have carefully gone over the page with your student and he has given the answers orally, he may then print the answers independently.

Note: In the second exercise on page 195, the word *guardian* may also be divided as **guard–i–an.**

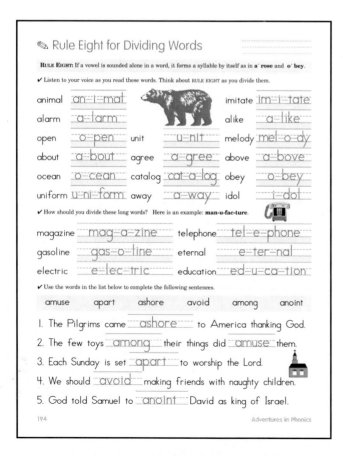

Page 196

Purpose

To review the first **Five Rules** for dividing words into syllables.

Lesson

As you discuss each rule one at a time, use the words under that rule for examples. Hopefully your student has learned much from these lessons on dividing words. These rules will also be reviewed in other grades, which will help him to gain a better understanding of them.

When you have carefully gone over the page and he has given the answers orally, he may then print the answers independently.

Page 197

Purpose

To review the last **Five Rules** for dividing words into syllables.

Lesson

As you discuss each rule one at a time, use the words under that rule for examples. Some of the rules are easier than others, but hopefully your student has learned much from these lessons on dividing words. These rules will also be reviewed in other grades, which will help him to gain a better understanding of them.

Under **Rules Six** and **Seven**, have the student divide the words in the boxes and print the correct words under their pictures. Under **Rules Eight**, **Nine** and **Ten**, have the student divide the words according to the respective rule being reviewed.

When you have carefully gone over the page and he has given the answers orally, he may then print the answers independently.

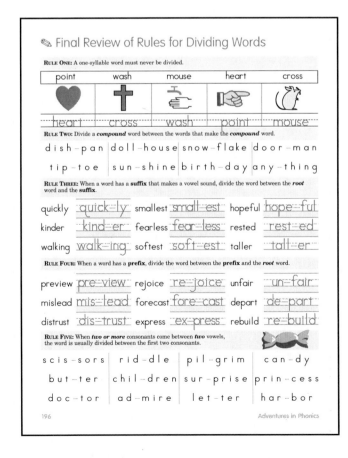

✎ Final Review of Rules for Dividing Words

RULE ONE: A one-syllable word must never be divided.

point	wash	mouse	heart	cross

heart   cross   wash   point   mouse

RULE TWO: Divide a *compound* word between the words that make the *compound* word.

d i s h – p a n | d o l l – h o u s e | s n o w – f l a k e | d o o r – m a n

t i p – t o e | s u n – s h i n e | b i r t h – d a y | a n y – t h i n g

RULE THREE: When a word has a **suffix** that makes a vowel sound, divide the word between the **root** word and the **suffix**.

quickly	quick–ly	smallest	small–est	hopeful	hope–ful
kinder	kind–er	fearless	fear–less	rested	rest–ed
walking	walk–ing	softest	soft–est	taller	tall–er

RULE FOUR: When a word has a **prefix**, divide the word between the **prefix** and the **root** word.

preview	pre–view	rejoice	re–joice	unfair	un–fair
mislead	mis–lead	forecast	fore–cast	depart	de–part
distrust	dis–trust	express	ex–press	rebuild	re–build

RULE FIVE: When *two or more* consonants come between *two* vowels, the word is usually divided between the first two consonants.

s c i s – s o r s | r i d – d l e | p i l – g r i m | c a n – d y

b u t – t e r | c h i l – d r e n | s u r – p r i s e | p r i n – c e s s

d o c – t o r | a d – m i r e | l e t – t e r | h a r – b o r

196   Adventures in Phonics

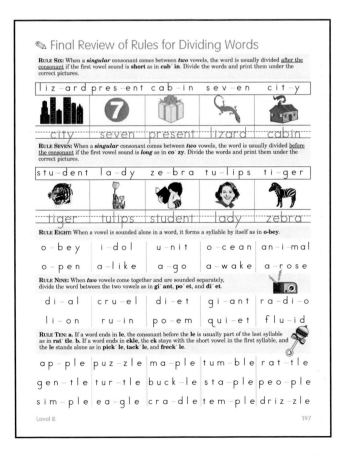

✎ Final Review of Rules for Dividing Words

RULE SIX: When a *singular* consonant comes between *two* vowels, the word is usually divided after the consonant if the first vowel sound is *short* as in cab´ in. Divide the words and print them under the correct pictures.

l i z – a r d | p r e s – e n t | c a b – i n | s e v – e n | c i t – y

city   seven   present   lizard   cabin

RULE SEVEN: When a *singular* consonant comes between *two* vowels, the word is usually divided before the consonant if the first vowel sound is *long* as in co´ zy. Divide the words and print them under the correct pictures.

s t u – d e n t | l a – d y | z e – b r a | t u – l i p s | t i – g e r

tiger   tulips   student   lady   zebra

RULE EIGHT: When a vowel is sounded alone in a word, it forms a syllable by itself as in o-bey.

o – b e y | i – d o l | u – n i t | o – c e a n | a n – i – m a l

o – p e n | a – l i k e | a – g o | a – w a k e | a – r o s e

RULE NINE: When *two* vowels come together and are sounded separately, divide the word between the two vowels as in gi´ ant, po´ et, and di´ et.

d i – a l | c r u – e l | d i – e t | g i – a n t | r a – d i – o

l i – o n | r u – i n | p o – e m | q u i – e t | f l u – i d

RULE TEN: a. If a word ends in **le**, the consonant before the **le** is usually part of the last syllable as in rat´ tle. b. If a word ends in **ckle**, the **ck** stays with the short vowel in the first syllable, and the **le** stands alone as in pick´ le, tack´ le, and freck´ le.

a p – p l e | p u z – z l e | m a – p l e | t u m – b l e | r a t – t l e

g e n – t l e | t u r – t l e | b u c k – l e | s t a – p l e | p e o – p l e

s i m – p l e | e a – g l e | c r a – d l e | t e m – p l e | d r i z – z l e

Level B   197

Page 198

Purpose
To teach the definition of a **synonym**.

Lesson
Discuss the definition of a synonym:

Words that have the **same** or a **similar** meaning.

Ask your student what words would mean the same as these that you say. There are several possible answers for many of the words.

happy	(glad)	**house**	(home)
close	(near)	**talk**	(speak)
woods	(forest)	**repair**	(fix)
shop	(store)	**quiet**	(still)

After you have carefully gone over the page with your student and he has given the answers orally, he may then print the answers independently.

Page 199

Purpose
To teach the definition of a **synonym**.

Lesson
Discuss the definition of a synonym:

Words that have the **same** or a **similar** meaning.

Ask your student what words would mean the same as these that you say. There are several possible answers for many of the words.

fall	(drop)	**child**	(infant)
small	(tiny)	**swift**	(fast)
level	(even)	**listen**	(hear)
store	(shop)	**funny**	(silly)

After you have carefully gone over the page with your student and he has given the answers orally, he may then print the answers independently.

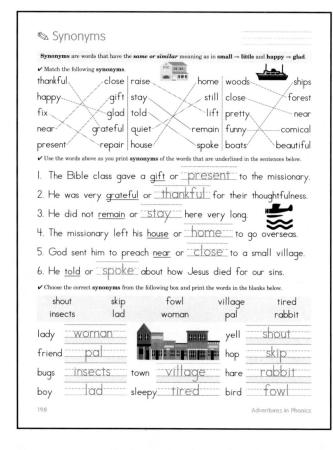

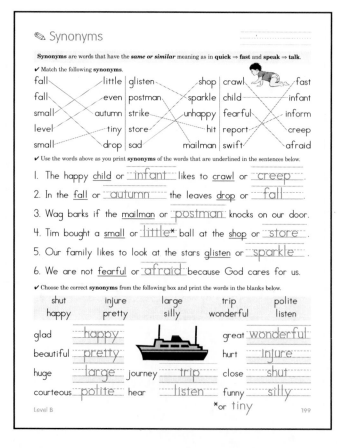

Page 200

Purpose
To teach the definition of an **antonym**.

Lesson
Discuss the definition of an antonym:

Words that have the **opposite** or **almost opposite** meaning.

Ask your student what words would have the opposite meaning of these words that you say. There are several possible answers for many of the words.

strong	(weak)	**wet**	(dry)
happy	(sad)	**light**	(dark)
near	(far)	**thick**	(thin)
many	(few)	**spend**	(save)

After you have carefully gone over the page with your student and he has given the answers orally, he may then print the answers independently.

Page 201

Purpose
To teach the definition of an **antonym**.

Lesson
Discuss the definition of an antonym:

Words that have the **opposite** or **almost opposite** meaning.

Ask your student what words would have the opposite meaning of these words that you say. There are several possible answers for many of the words.

under	(over)	**asleep**	(awake)
fast	(slow)	**go**	(come)
hot	(cold)	**hard**	(soft)
young	(old)	**lose**	(win)

After you have carefully gone over the page with your student and he has given the answers orally, he may then print the answers independently.

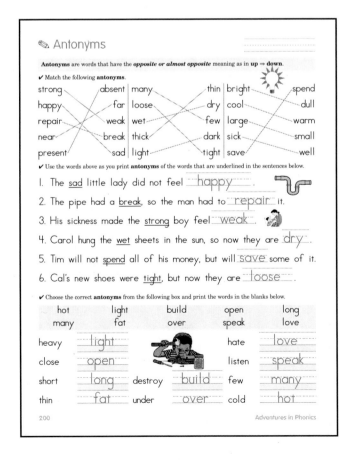

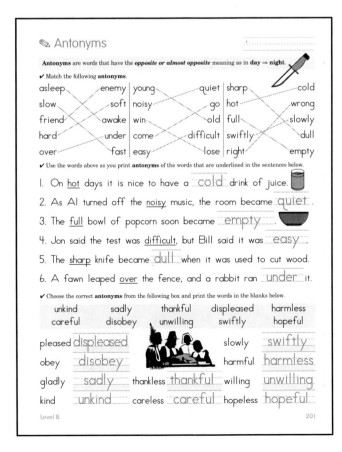

Page 202

Purpose

To review the definitions of **synonyms** and **antonyms**.

Lesson

Discuss both of the definitions. Go slowly through the lesson, giving sufficient time for the student to think about the words he is comparing.

After you have carefully gone over the page with your student and he has given the answers orally, he may then complete the answers independently.

Page 203

Purpose

To teach the definition of a **homonym**.

Lesson

Discuss the definition of a homonym:

> Words that **sound alike**, but have a different meaning and spelling.

Ask your student to fill in the correct homonyms in the following sets of sentences.

My dress is *blue.*

The wind _____.

The ball went *through* the hoop.

Bill _____ the ball to me.

Talk about the meaning of these homonyms.

peek	peak	break	brake
road	rode	weigh	way

After you have carefully discussed the page with your student and he has given the answers orally, he may then complete the answers independently.

✎ Review of Synonyms and Antonyms

Synonyms are words that have the *same or similar* meaning as in **small ⇒ little**.
Antonyms are words that have the *opposite or almost opposite* meaning as in **up ⇒ down**.

✔ In the blanks between the words, print an **S** if the words are **synonyms**, words that have the *same* meaning, or print an **A** if the words are **antonyms**, words that have the *opposite* meaning.

good	A	bad	foolish	A	wise	report	S	tell
quiet	S	still	big	S	large	hate	A	love
inside	A	outside	joy	A	sadness	high	A	low
tall	A	short	idea	S	plan	in	A	out
over	A	under	quick	S	swift	go	S	leave
rush	S	hurry	hot	A	cold	sick	S	ill
under	S	below	protect	S	guard	happy	A	unhappy
shut	S	close	up	A	down	kind	A	mean

✔ Complete these sentences with these **synonyms and antonyms**.

wise	beautiful	outside	kindly	ascend	sparkle

1. If you are not <u>inside</u> your home, you are outside of it.

2. The <u>pretty</u> dress looked beautiful on the little girl.

3. The stars look like they <u>glisten</u> or sparkle in the sky.

4. The way of a <u>fool</u> seems right to him, but a wise man listens to advice. (see Proverbs 12:15)

5. We should not speak <u>evil</u> but kindly toward others.

6. Andy likes to watch planes <u>climb</u> or ascend into the sky.

202   Adventures in Phonics

✎ Homonyms

Homonyms are words that *sound alike*, but have *different* meanings and spellings as in **deer ⇒ dear**.

✔ Match the following **homonyms**.

1. maid	3	sent	1. weak	3	won	1. bee	3	seam
2. blew	4	rode	2. through	5	beet	2. meet	5	would
3. cent	1	made	3. one	1	week	3. seem	4	do
4. road	5	write	4. eight	2	threw	4. dew	1	be
5. right	2	blue	5. beat	4	ate	5. wood	2	meat

✔ Choose the correct **homonym** from the box at the right to complete each of the following sentences.

1. Al helped his mother peel apples for a pie. | peal | peel
2. The wind blew some sand into our faces. | blue | blew
3. Some sand got into Tim's left eye. | I | eye
4. Bill's weight has gone up ten pounds. | wait | weight
5. Bob hiked to the peak of the mountain. | peak | peek
6. His nose got red from the sunshine. | nose | knows
7. He was happy as he rode down in a car. | road | rode

✔ Match the following homonyms.

1. our	2	read	1. or	3	wrap	1. pain	2	lead
2. red	4	flour	2. ring	4	knot	2. led	4	sale
3. fare	1	hour	3. rap	1	oar	3. feet	1	pane
4. flower	3	fair	4. not	2	wring	4. sail	3	feat

Level B   203

Page 204

Purpose

To teach the three possible sounds of the digraph **ch**.

To give additional practice in adding the suffix **-ed** and saying the sound it makes as it is added to a short vowel sound word.

Lesson

Discuss the three sounds of **ch** as they are mentioned in the directions. Many of the **ch** words may be new to your student. Go slowly through the lesson as he gives you the answers. If the student has questions about the sound of the suffix **-ed**, refer to page 140 in the workbook or page 70 in this teacher's guide.

When you feel your student is ready, ask him to complete the written work independently.

Page 205

Purpose

To teach the sounds of the digraphs **gh** and **ph**.

Lesson

Introduce these sounds and listen to your student read the words in Chart 43 (page 228 in the workbook). You may also use the **ph** flashcard.

Many of the words in this lesson will be new to your student. Go slowly through the lists and exercises as he tells you the answers.

When you feel your student is ready, ask him to complete the written work independently.

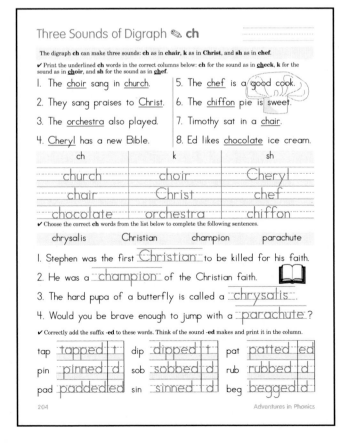

Three Sounds of Digraph ✎ ch

The digraph **ch** can make three sounds: **ch** as in **chair**, **k** as in **Christ**, and **sh** as in **chef**.

✔ Print the underlined **ch** words in the correct columns below: **ch** for the sound as in **check**, **k** for the sound as in **choir**, and **sh** for the sound as in **chef**.

1. The <u>choir</u> sang in <u>church</u>.
2. They sang praises to <u>Christ</u>.
3. The <u>orchestra</u> also played.
4. <u>Cheryl</u> has a new Bible.
5. The <u>chef</u> is a good cook.
6. The <u>chiffon</u> pie is sweet.
7. Timothy sat in a <u>chair</u>.
8. Ed likes <u>chocolate</u> ice cream.

ch	k	sh
church	choir	Cheryl
chair	Christ	chef
chocolate	orchestra	chiffon

✔ Choose the correct **ch** words from the list below to complete the following sentences.

chrysalis	Christian	champion	parachute

1. Stephen was the first Christian to be killed for his faith.
2. He was a champion of the Christian faith.
3. The hard pupa of a butterfly is called a chrysalis.
4. Would you be brave enough to jump with a parachute?

✔ Correctly add the suffix **-ed** to these words. Think of the sound **-ed** makes and print it in the column.

tap	tapped	t	dip	dipped	t	pat	patted	ed
pin	pinned	d	sob	sobbed	d	rub	rubbed	d
pad	paddded	d	sin	sinned	d	beg	begged	d

204   Adventures in Phonics

Digraphs ✎ gh and ph

The digraphs **gh** and **ph** can make the sound of **f** as in **digraph**, **phrase**, **laugh**, and **tough**.

✔ Print the **gh** and **ph** words under their correct pictures.

telephone	cough	photo	dolphin	elephant
elephant	dolphin	telephone	photo	cough

Review the following digraphs: **ch, sh, th, wh, kn, gn, wr, ph, gh,** and **ck**.

✔ Circle the **digraphs** in these words. Use the underlined words to complete the sentences below.

Christ	parachute	which	knock	chef
rough	telephone	shepherd	chocolate	Philip
birthday	thick	sign	church	champion
Phyllis	together	chorus	thermometer	whisper
tough	brother	sheep	knowledge	laugh

1. The Lord is the shepherd of his people.
2. The girls' chorus sang about the birth of Christ.
3. Mom used a thermometer to see if I had a fever.
4. Grandpa called the twins Philip and Phyllis.
5. They like to talk together on the telephone.
6. The twins each got a big chocolate candy bar.
7. Charlie knows that it is wrong to whisper in church.

Level B   205

Page 206

Purpose
To teach about the suffix -tion.

Lesson
The suffix **-tion** modifies or changes a root word to help it have a special meaning or use. The **-tion** makes the sound of *shun*.

Read and discuss these words with your student.

create	creation
invent	invention
elect	election
inject	injection
introduce	introduction
celebrate	celebration
educate	education

Many of the words in this lesson will be new to him. Go slowly through the lists and exercises as he tells you the answers.

When you feel your student is ready, ask him to complete the written work independently.

Page 207

Purpose
To teach about the suffix -sion.

Lesson
The suffix **-sion** modifies or changes a root word to help it have a special meaning or use. The **-sion** makes the sound of *shun* or *zhun.*

Read and discuss these words with your student.

collide	collision
discuss	discussion
divide	division
admit	admission
exclude	exclusion
revise	revision
conclude	conclusion

Many of the words in this lesson will be new to him. Go slowly through the lists and exercises as he tells you the answers.

When you feel your student is ready, ask him to complete the written work independently.

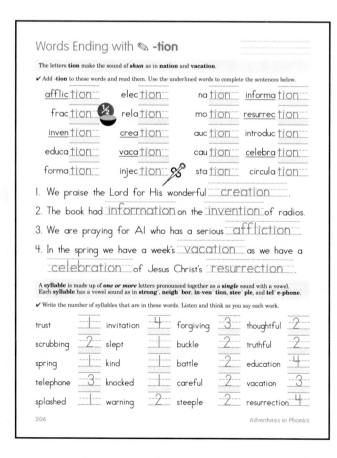

Words Ending with ✎ -tion

The letters **tion** make the sound of *shun* as in **nation** and **vacation**.

✔ Add **-tion** to these words and read them. Use the underlined words to complete the sentences below.

afflic tion	elec tion	na tion	informa tion
frac tion	rela tion	mo tion	resurrec tion
inven tion	crea tion	auc tion	introduc tion
educa tion	vaca tion	cau tion	celebra tion
forma tion	injec tion	sta tion	circula tion

1. We praise the Lord for His wonderful __creation__.
2. The book had __information__ on the __invention__ of radios.
3. We are praying for Al who has a serious __affliction__.
4. In the spring we have a week's __vacation__ as we have a __celebration__ of Jesus Christ's __resurrection__.

A **syllable** is made up of *one or more* letters pronounced together as a *single* sound with a vowel. Each **syllable** has a vowel sound as in **strong´, neigh´bor, in-ven´tion, stee´ple,** and **tel´e-phone.**

✔ Write the number of syllables that are in these words. Listen and think as you say each work.

trust	1	invitation	4	forgiving	3	thoughtful	2
scrubbing	2	slept	1	buckle	2	truthful	2
spring	1	kind	1	battle	2	education	4
telephone	3	knocked	1	careful	2	vacation	3
splashed	1	warning	2	steeple	2	resurrection	4

206   Adventures in Phonics

Words Ending with ✎ -sion

The letters **-sion** make the sound of *shun* or *zhun* as in **discussion** and **division**.

✔ Add **-sion** to these words and read them. Use the underlined words to complete the sentences below.

colli sion	admis sion	conclu sion	televi sion
discus sion	exclu sion	inva sion	confu sion
divi sion	revi sion	excur sion	fu sion

1. You have had many hours of talking or __discussion__.
2. It is better to read a book than to watch __television__.
3. Terry was glad that the story had a happy __conclusion__.
4. There was __confusion__ as the children looked for their shoes.
5. We prayed for a friend who was in a car __collision__.
6. Children under ten paid no __admission__ to the fair.

Do you remember that sometimes digraphs **gh** and **ph** make the sound of **f** as in **laugh** and **telephone**? Do you also remember that the digraph **ch** makes three different sounds as in **chip, chef,** and **choir**?

✔ Use the words in the list below to complete the following sentences.

| elephant | chauffeur | phonics | spinach | rough |

1. A __chauffeur__ came to take the bride to church.
2. God made something like a finger at the end of the trunk of an __elephant__. Would it like to eat __spinach__?
3. Philip enjoyed reading because he learned __phonics__.
4. The hard-working farmer had very strong, __rough__ hands.

Level B   207

Page 208

Purpose

To review words having different sounds of the vowel **o**.

Lesson

As the directions say, this lesson includes three of the sounds of the vowel **o**. Read the lines of words several times to help your student to know the sounds well.

ô	ŏ	ō
soft	shop	home
dog	rock	comb
frog	pond	low
cloth	drop	goat
off	sob	own

Review the rule about changing the **y** to **i** before adding **-ed** to words ending with a **y** next to a consonant. Don't change the **y** when it is next to a vowel.

After you have gone over the entire lesson with your student and you feel he is ready, ask him to complete the written work independently.

Page 209

Purpose

To review the two rules for using the **apostrophe**.

Lesson

Follow the directions as they discuss the rules one at a time. Use the examples on the lesson as you review.

After you have gone over the entire lesson with your student and you feel he is ready, ask him to complete the written work independently.

Hopefully, you both can see an improvement in his printing.

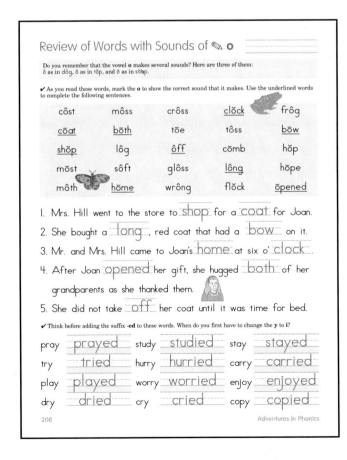

Review of Words with Sounds of ✎ o

Do you remember that the vowel o makes several sounds? Here are three of them: ô as in dôg, ŏ as in tŏp, and ō as in sōap.

✔ As you read these words, mark the o to show the correct sound that it makes. Use the underlined words to complete the following sentences.

côst	môss	crôss	clŏck	frôg
cōat	bōth	tōe	tôss	bōw
shŏp	lôg	ôff	cōmb	hŏp
mōst	sôft	glôss	lông	hōpe
môth	hōme	wrông	flŏck	ōpened

1. Mrs. Hill went to the store to <u>shop</u> for a <u>coat</u> for Joan.

2. She bought a <u>long</u>, red coat that had a <u>bow</u> on it.

3. Mr. and Mrs. Hill came to Joan's <u>home</u> at six o' <u>clock</u>.

4. After Joan <u>opened</u> her gift, she hugged <u>both</u> of her grandparents as she thanked them.

5. She did not take <u>off</u> her coat until it was time for bed.

✔ Think before adding the suffix **-ed** to these words. When do you first have to change the y to i?

pray	prayed	study	studied	stay	stayed
try	tried	hurry	hurried	carry	carried
play	played	worry	worried	enjoy	enjoyed
dry	dried	cry	cried	copy	copied

208   Adventures in Phonics

✎ Review of the Apostrophe

The little mark called the **apostrophe** (') is used in two ways.
RULE 1: To show that someone or something *owns or possesses* something, an **apostrophe** and an **s** ('s) is added to the end of the word as in **the cat's dish**.

✔ Add 's to show possession or ownership.

ball of Dale	Dale's ball	dog of Connel	Connel's dog
doll of Tara	Tara's doll	suit of Eric	Eric's suit
truck of Calvin	Calvin's truck	bed of baby	baby's bed
dress of Jane	Jane's dress	quilt of Mary	Mary's quilt
book of Jim	Jim's book	rug of Kelsey	Kelsey's rug

A **contraction** is a short way of writing two words. As they are written together, *one or more* letters are left out. Here is the second way in which the little mark called the **apostrophe** (') is used.
RULE 2: An apostrophe is put in the place of the missing letters. Usually the first word is not changed.

do not ⇒ **don't**   they will ⇒ **they'll**   he is ⇒ **he's**   you are ⇒ **you're**   we have ⇒ **we've**

✔ Take out the underlined letters. Add an **apostrophe** (') where the letters are removed: let us ⇒ **let's**.

we <u>have</u>	we've	they <u>are</u>	they're	has <u>not</u>	hasn't
would <u>not</u>	wouldn't	let <u>us</u>	let's	he <u>is</u>	he's
we <u>are</u>	we're	have <u>not</u>	haven't	they <u>will</u>	they'll
it <u>will</u>	it'll	you <u>have</u>	you've	it <u>is</u>	it's
she <u>will</u>	she'll	here <u>is</u>	here's	we <u>will</u>	we'll
they <u>have</u>	they've	could <u>not</u>	couldn't	are <u>not</u>	aren't
should <u>not</u>	shouldn't	she <u>is</u>	she's	he <u>will</u>	he'll

✔ Print the words that are in these **contractions**.

they've = they have   here's = here is   haven't = have not

Level B   209

Page 210

Purpose
To review the definitions of **synonyms**, **antonyms**, and **homonyms**.

Lesson
Carefully discuss the definitions of these three big words with easy meanings.

After you have slowly gone over the entire lesson with your student and you feel he is ready, ask him to complete the written work independently.

Page 211

Purpose
To review words with the short vowel sound of **u** that is made by **o** and **a**.

Lesson
After you have gone over this lesson with your student and you feel he is ready, ask him to complete the written work independently.

✎ Synonyms, Antonyms, and Homonyms

Synonyms are words that have the *same or similar* meaning as in **small ⇒ little**.
Antonyms are words that have the *opposite or almost opposite* meanings as in **in ⇒ out**.
Homonyms are words that *sound alike*, but have *different* meanings and spellings as in **be ⇒ bee**.

✔ In the blanks between the words, print an **S** if the words are **synonyms**, words that have the *same* meaning; print an **A** if the words are **antonyms**, words that have the *opposite* meanings; or print **H** if the words are **homonyms**, words that *sound alike* but have *different* meanings and spellings.

soft	A	rough	foolish	A	wise		
protect	S	guard	big	S	large		
weight	H	wait	tight	A	loose	repair	S	fix
careful	A	careless	blue	H	blew	present	A	absent
under	S	below	lost	A	found	through	H	threw
light	A	dark	sick	S	ill	strong	A	weak
rode	H	road	thought	S	idea	shut	A	open
go	S	leave	see	H	sea	quick	A	slow

✔ Complete these sentences with these **synonyms** and **antonyms**.

quickly   Woods   noisy   building   glistened   journey

1. The boys enjoyed hiking in the <u>forest</u> called Butler Woods.

2. At times it was <u>quiet</u>, but sometimes it was quite noisy.

3. They went on a <u>trip</u> or journey through the forest.

4. A rabbit hopping <u>slowly</u>, suddenly went quickly away.

5. They watched as a bird was <u>making</u> or building its nest.

6. A little brook <u>sparkled</u> or glistened as they hiked past it.

210   Adventures in Phonics

Words with Short Vowel Sound of ✎ u

The vowel **o** sometimes has the <u>short vowel</u> sound of **u** as in **mother**, **shovel**, and **dove**.

✔ Print these short vowel **o** words under the correct pictures.

glove	shovel	oven	money	dove
money	dove	shovel	oven	glove

✔ Use these words to complete the following sentences.

| month | done | come | mother | some |
| brother | other | son | loving | nothing |

1. Victor and his younger brother have just come inside.

2. They have done their homework. What should they do now?

3. It is the month of April so the weather is warm.

4. They try to be kind and loving to each other.

5. Their father and mother are so thankful for them.

6. Did you ever have a day when you had nothing to do?

7. The older son has some paper they will color.

The vowel **a** has the *schwa* sound or <u>short vowel</u> sound of **u** as in **ago** and **away**.

✔ Divide these words. How quickly can you read them? Put the accent mark after the last syllable.

a-rose'	a-sleep'	a-bide'	a-shore'	a-dorn'
a-like'	a-noint'	a-loud'	a-gree'	a-new'
a-wait'	a-bout'	a-gain'	a-while'	a-head'

Level B   211

Page 212

Purpose

To introduce the student to *alphabetizing* words from a list. To use a **dictionary** to find the meaning of words the student does not know.

Lesson

Note that the two lists at the bottom of the page should be alphabetized separately.

After you have gone over this lesson with your student and you feel he is ready, ask him to complete the written work independently.

Page 213

Purpose

To introduce the student to *alphabetizing* words from a list. To use a **dictionary** to find the meaning of words the student does not know.

Lesson

Note that the two lists at the top of the page should be alphabetized separately. However, at the bottom of the page, the student should alphabetize both lists together. Explain that the three words *hands*, *head*, and *heart* are placed according the second or fourth letters in the words.

After you have gone over this lesson with your student and you feel he is ready, ask him to complete the written work independently.

✎ Words in Alphabetical Order

Do you know what the word **raiment** means? How would you use a **tambourine**?
A good place to look for answers is in a **dictionary**. The words are arranged in alphabetical order, so they are easily found. You can learn about many words as you study a **dictionary**.

a b c d e f g h i j k l m n o p q r s t u v w x y z

These words are written in **alphabetical order**. The word beginning with **a** is written first.

| apple | basket | cross | deer | envelope | fish | gift |

If you do not have words that begin with each letter, just skip the letter and go to the next word.

| boat | desk | elephant | flake | heart | seal | tools |

✔ Number these papers in **alphabetical order**. REMEMBER: Skip letters that are not used.

Hannah	Adam	Benjamin	Daniel	Grace	Elizabeth	Connel
7	1	2	4	6	5	3

✔ Number these recipe cards in **alphabetical order**. REMEMBER: All the letters may not be there.

breads	vegetables	desserts	cookies	appetizers	meats	salads
2	7	4	3	1	5	6

✔ Put these words in **alphabetical order**. Think about the alphabet. You may look up at the top.

wagon	bicycle		lemonade	apples
swing	helmet		salad	chicken
bicycle	swing		apples	lemonade
helmet	wagon	Let's have a picnic!	chicken	salad

212   Adventures in Phonics

✎ Words in Alphabetical Order

A Christian man named **Noah Webster** was the first American to produce a good **dictionary**. It was printed in 1828. He worked very hard and spent a great deal of time to organize this important book. It is such a helpful book for us, so we need to learn how to use it properly.

a b c d e f g h i j k l m n o p q r s t u v w x y z

✔ Think of the alphabet; look at the first letter of each word. Put the words in **alphabetical order**.

jet	boat	rabbit	giraffe
boat	cab	kangaroo	kangaroo
helicopter	helicopter	panda	panda
cab	jet	squirrel	rabbit
train	train	giraffe	squirrel

Some words begin with the same letter, such as **Connel** and **Calvin**. We then need to look at the **second** letter to see which word should come **first** in the dictionary: **C**o**nnel** or **C**a**lvin**? The letter **a** comes before **o**. The name **Calvin** would come before **Connel** in a dictionary.

✔ Think about the **second** letter as you alphabetize these names that begin with the same letter.

| D**o**ris | 2 | S**a**muel | 1 | B**o**bby | 2 | T**i**mmy | 1 | A**n**na | 2 |
| D**a**nny | 1 | S**u**san | 2 | B**i**lly | 1 | T**o**mmy | 2 | A**l**ex | 1 |

✔ Carefully alphabetize all the words in both lists. NOTE: Some of them begin with the same letter.

feet	arms		head	head
hands	ears		soul	heart
legs	eyes		eyes	legs
arms	feet	I will praise Thee: for I am fearfully and wonderfully made. . Psalms 139:14	mouth	mouth
heart	hands		ears	soul

Level B   213